How To Become A State Wrestling Champion

Learn Proven Strategies To:

Think like a warrior
Intimidate your opponents
Win more matches
Score more points
Train for success
Develop more confidence

Charles A. Martelli

Copyright © 2002 by Charles A. Martelli
All rights reserved. This book may not be reproduced in whole or in part without permission.

Library of Congress Control Number: 2002095803

ISBN 0-9726395-0-0

Pictures by:
Front Cover: Chris Vivio
Back Cover: Ed Bankowski

Published by:
State Champion Wrestling Company
1404 West St.
Naperville, Il 60563
www.statechampwrestling.com

Cover design by:
L Communications
Evanston, IL

Printed by:
Color House Graphics
Grand Rapids, MI

Edited by:
Jessie Veith
Bob Chenoweth

For my parents, who have weathered the winds of my many storms through strength and dedication, and who have helped me to always come out victorious.

A special dedication goes out to "The Club." You guys are an amazing group of dedicated friends.

Table Of Contents

Acknowledgments	ix
Preface: A Note To The Reader	1
Introduction: A Father's Reluctant Confession	7
Step One: Working Smart	15
Step Two: One-on-One Not Two-On-One	31
Step Three: Adopting A Winning Wrestling Style	43
Step Four: Goal Setting	57
Step Five: Drilling	71
Step Six: Visualization Plus	79
Camps and Clinics	87
The Wrap-Up	97

How To Become A State Wrestling Champion

Acknowledgments

Throughout my wrestling career I always set lofty goals I knew could only be achieved through great dedication and lots of smart, hard work. I knew that when push came to shove that I was working harder than all of my competition around the country. I was putting in more hours watching film, lifting, drilling, and traveling to find the best coaching.

However, I know that I could not have been as dedicated as I was to wrestling or worked as hard as I had without a large support staff of family, friends, coaches, and teammates to help me stay on the right path. While there were hundreds of people who helped me in one capacity or another as I worked towards winning my state titles, there were a few individuals who impacted my wrestling career in a more significant manner. Without them, I would not be able to look back on my championships with the great pride and self-respect that I do.

First and foremost, a giant thank you goes to my family, whom I feel is the backbone of my life. You are my world and there are not enough words to express my gratitude and love for you.

To those who were with me at the beginning, I say thanks to the coaches of the

A proven plan that guarantees success.

Patriot Wrestling Club for lighting the spark to my wrestling career. A special thank you to Cris Pradel who always believed I was a winner and supported me to the end.

Coach Nutt and Coach Geyer of Jefferson Junior High were always there to push me to the next level in my early years. Both were selfless in their mission to develop confidence in young athletes while pushing them to be their best. Thanks for your early support that laid the groundwork for my state titles.

The coaching staff at Naperville North High School from 1994-1998 had a great impact on both my wrestling career and my growing up as a person. Thank you to Rob Williams, Cory Anderson, Mike Meluch, John Meyers, Wayne Miller, Dave Bendis, and Dave Andrews. You were always by my side for support, motivation, a good story, and a great laugh or two. A special thanks to Coach Tom Arlis, my head coach for four years, who knew from the start that I could do great things. When he heard that my goal in sophomore year was simply to qualify for the state tournament he replied, "Qualify? This kid is going to place." It is this sort of belief in my ability that guided me to two state finals and two state titles with him in the corner. Thank you for your belief, confidence, and vision of my talents. Without them, I would not have accomplished what I set out to do.

Tom Champion was the secret to my success. His One-on-One training allowed me to catch up to the competition that had years of experience on me. His unselfishness and hunger for the sport of wrestling pushed me to levels I never knew I could reach. Thank you for your skills, talents, and most of all friendship.

How to become the next state wrestling champion.

Dan Knight and Andy Rein were two individuals who were 100% willing to give me some of their knowledge of sport whether it was technique based or experience based. They gave me a large arsenal of moves to build my style around. Without their One-on-One help, I could not have developed into the well-rounded wrestler I became. Thank you for taking the time to share your knowledge and love for the sport with me.

The coaching staff from the University of Michigan recruited me and gave me the opportunity to compete at a Division I level while earning a college degree. Joe McFarland, Dale Bahr, Kirk Trost, Sean Bormet, Tony Robie, Kevin Vogel, John Fischer, and Ed Bankowski are the greatest group of coaches I have ever been involved with. I have had the distinct opportunity to work with each one of these coaches during my four years at U of M and each one added their own piece of the puzzle to my career. Although they all have their own separate expert areas of technique and experience, they share a common vision of hard work, dedication, and thirst for victory. Thank you for your belief, honesty, and dedication to helping me get to the next level.

Without the help of each and every teammate I have had I would not have been able to accomplish my goals. Somehow I always managed to find myself on a team surrounded with dedicated and team-oriented athletes. My teammates at U of M defined the words *friend* and *teammate* by being there for me anytime, anyplace. They could not have made my transition from a great high school team to a great college team more memorable. Thank you all.

I realize that there are many more people that I need to thank, and will sometime on a face-

A proven plan that guarantees success.

to-face basis, but these are the coaches and supporters that have had the greatest impact on my career as a wrestler and person. Once again, thanks to everyone who lent a helping hand in my quest for success.

Preface

A Note To The Reader

"Your attitude, not your aptitude, will determine your altitude."

-*Zig Ziglar*

In June of 2002, I completed my fourth year of undergraduate studies at one of the most prestigious universities in the world, the University of Michigan, and never for one moment wanted to be anywhere else. Every day I was challenged inside of the classroom, competing with top-notch students from around the world and outside of the classroom through wrestling top-notch athletes from around the country. Deciding to attend the University of Michigan my senior year of high school was the best decision I ever made. Everything that I had learned from wrestling up to that point combined to give me the opportunity of a lifetime. Wrestling at Michigan allowed me to build on each aspect of

A proven plan that guarantees success.

my wrestling—and life as well— through the hard work and discipline that Michigan required and expected.

I had the distinct privilege of not only competing for one of the United States' best wrestling programs, but I was able to compete for four straight years. Competing on the University of Michigan's varsity wrestling squad for four years is a rare and unique accomplishment. Additionally, doing it at a Division I school is even more uncommon. Wrestling at Michigan provided me with the opportunity to compete against the best wrestlers in the country, every week, and allowed me to walk out of a world-renowned school with a degree that has precedent. I could not ask for anything more. Although the book you are about to read is not about college, I feel it is important I give you a hint of where my successful high school wrestling career took me.

This book is indeed about high school. More specifically, it focuses on the most important, crucial steps needed to become a high school **state champion**. I include in this preface a short reference to my college career because by following the steps we outline here, **I WAS ABLE TO RECEIVE A COLLEGE EDUCATION AND YOU MAY BE ABLE TO DO THE SAME.** If it had not been for the principles and philosophies adopted by my father, my family and I, this book would never have been written to guide you on your mission to the awards podium. The information within these chapters describes proven strategies that have brought me success, a college education, and helped me learn how to overcome all types of obstacles along the way to my championships.

The sport of wrestling is by no means an easy or gentle sport. It is the world's oldest and best sport that requires a person to have a complete package of techniques, excellent mental preparation, and physical skills to become successful. This is not a sport that any individual can succeed in, but it is certainly a sport that any individual can take part in. The young, weak, and small all have an equal opportunity to work towards winning a state title. The only thing that is going to separate the weak from the strong and the timid from the brave is a successful step-by-step game plan.

    A game plan is like a recipe. There is a list of ingredients that all contribute to the overall outcome of the final product. Technique, strength, emotion, attitude, and morals are just a few of the ingredients that make the final product, a **state championship**, possible.

    Throughout your journey in the sport of wrestling you will come across hundreds of obstacles and people who will try to get in your way. It is up to you to knock down these barriers and forge ahead. I have experienced time and time again parents, referees, coaches and wrestlers who were determined not to let me succeed. I refused to say die. I refused to back off. I was relentless in my pursuit of victory. I used my opponent's energy as my fuel. I turned their pessimism (negative attitude) towards me into my optimism (positive attitude).

    Winning state titles was my goal and I was not going to let outsiders get in the way of my dreams. I had a game plan, a work ethic, and a support system on my side. By combining each of the ingredients found in this book, I was able to accomplish my goal and win two state titles. I was also able to take a third place in state my sophomore year, where my only losses were to two **state champions**. In my senior year I became

A proven plan that guarantees success.

a high school All-American and was Naperville North High School's athlete of the year. These are just a few of the same major accomplishments that you will be able to seize by using our game plan and sticking to it.

If you follow my lead and the recipe that my father and I have developed you too will become a **state champion**. It is crucial that you not only read the black ink that fills these pages, but also that you allow it seep deep into your mind. You must make the messages part of your subconscious. Open your mind and be open to suggestions and change. You will notice as you move forward through the "six essential strategies" (parts) that there are several main themes that we hit on. Change is one of the biggest, so familiarize yourself with it now.

Realize that I am proof that you can accomplish what you set out to do. I did not start wrestling until the sixth grade, at the age of twelve, and was well behind my peers. Many of the kids I met along my journey had been wrestling since they were in diapers, literally. However, this disadvantage was not a threat to my dreams, but rather a challenge. The challenge was to find a way to make up for lost time. My dad and I developed our philosophies and principles out of necessity. With the odds stacked against me, I was put to a test and needed to make a choice. Was I willing to make a commitment to accomplish my dreams? You must ask yourself this same question as I did as a twelve-year-old kid without a lick of wrestling background, "Am I willing to change and make a commitment?"

Once you decide you are willing to put in the time, you will find your journey tremendously gratifying and self-fulfilling. You will come out on top of the awards podium with the gold medal dangling from your neck. It will be a symbol of greatness, for you will be the champion. Ten thousand people will raise to their feet screaming, chanting, clapping, and praising you. The culmination of years of smart work, hard work, and dedication will combine in a span of ten seconds when your hand is raised in victory. The thrill of victory will never be sweeter than at the moment of reflection.

The moment in which you are able to freeze time inside your mind, applause and cheers will be like no other. The years of sweat, toil, and pain will be ever vivid on the forefront of your mind. For a split second a tear of joy will ball in the corner of your eye. Before you realize it, that tear is accentuated by a loud cry of triumph as your hand is raised high and your index finger is outstretched symbolizing number one. **YOU WILL BE NUMBER ONE FOR A SINGLE MOMENT IN TIME, AND NO ONE WILL EVER BE ABLE TO TAKE THAT AWAY FROM YOU. FOR THE REST OF YOUR LIFE YOU WILL BE THE BEST AT YOUR WEIGHT THAT YEAR. YOU WILL KNOW YOU HAVE EARNED EVERY BIT OF IT. GO FOR IT!!!**

I had the honor of feeling these rare and gratifying emotions twice. It can be done! Get out and do it and never look back. Whether you come from a long history of wrestling champions or you and your family are newcomers to the sport, seek and destroy. Adopt our game plan and become the **state champion** I know you can be. You might even find yourself there more than once. Good luck on your mission.

You will notice that we breakdown a number of important themes and topics several times. This is to ensure that they stick in your mind for good. Don't be afraid to look back on this book during your journey to the podium. Use this book as the cookbook, filled with recipes and ingredients that will produce the most perfect result imaginable. Take notes in the margins of the pages, highlight pages, and absorb the images of victory. Someday it will be you experiencing success that you can carry with you for the rest of your life.

"A good plan vigorously executed right now is far better than a perfect plan executed next week."
    - General George S. Patton, Jr.

Introduction

A Father's Reluctant Confession

Starting out with a brief confession never hurt anyone. I feel that if I tell the truth of our experience from the start, we will both feel a lot better later on.

It seems like only yesterday, my son was in the sixth grade. It was in the late fall and football season was coming to a close. I can hear myself saying to my son, "They do not have wrestling for your age group (twelve years). Anyway, why would you want to wrestle? Don't you have enough to do with swimming, baseball, soccer, football, and basketball?" Does this conversation sound familiar at all?

There was no way we could fit wrestling into my son's already packed schedule. Apparently he had started wrestling in gym class one afternoon and was especially excited to get started on a team. He talked me into contacting the local high school coach and, as they say, the rest is history. That same year basketball, swimming, soccer, and baseball became sports of the past. Wrestling was Charles' new favorite pastime.

Oh yeah, about my confession. It is hard to admit, but neither my son nor I had ever seen a wrestling match or even gone to a wrestling meet. Come to think of it, no one in our family had ever gone to one either. As it turned out, our lack of knowledge about the sport was a great advantage for us. We had no preconceived notions that could have interfered with giving our son the go-ahead to become a wrestler.

We did not know of the problems involved with cutting weight, cauliflower ears and how they get that way, or even how brutal the sport can be. We knew absolutely nothing about the sport.

However, the one thing we did know was how to succeed in other areas of life, and we took these experiences, the basic building blocks of living, so to speak, and put them into play on our wrestling journey.

Anyone could see that Chuck liked the sport of wrestling right away. One clue was that he always came home from practice with more enthusiasm than when he had left for practice. I would ask him questions such as, "How was practice tonight, son?" His answer would always be something along the lines of, "Practice was great, awesome. We worked on..." I could never get over the fact that someone could not only enjoy a sport but actually enjoy practice as well.

Wrestler Qualifications

Like anything else in life, to become a **state champion** you need some basic qualifications. You do not need to be a great athlete but you do need to be an athlete who has the burning desire to be great. Along with that burning desire you will need the following key elements:

- An open mind with the willingness to change
- A work ethic that will enable you to stick to something until the task is complete
- A support team made up of family members, coaches, teachers, friends, teammates and drill partners. They will become invaluable as you start to use our plan of attack.

"Winners can tell you where they are going, what they plan to do along the way and who will be sharing the adventure with them."
- Denis Waitley

Fundamentals

It is important to us that you understand two things: first, why we decided to help you accomplish your dream of becoming a **state champion** and second, why we feel our plan for becoming a champion works.

My son and I decided to put our thoughts down on paper because we felt the need to give something back to a sport that has given him and our family countless opportunities. I personally enjoy wrestling more than any other sport that my son has been involved with, which has made writing this book a wonderful experience.

To all of the families that have a child involved with wrestling, some of whom are still trying to win that first match and want their

A proven plan that guarantees success.

wrestler to succeed, I would like to give you a message. We know of your pain because we have been on both sides of winning and losing. I vividly remember one boy on our kids' club team I personally helped out with, but who never won a match. Not a single match. I can still feel his pain to this day.

The plan that Charles and I have outlined and the things we have learned about becoming a **state champion** will be of great benefit to those who choose to read and implement the plan. If it worked for my son, without a single iota of wrestling experience, we know it can and will work for you.

Alongside this book are a lot of other good books about wrestling, but most of them are either about wrestling techniques or are biographies about a particular successful wrestler. This book is neither. It is much different because it tells exactly what you need to do to become the champion that lies within you. We know you can become a **state champion** by using this book as your "planning guide" because we have done it.

Now that you know a little about the approach to this book it is time to start thinking about changing your life. Take control of your future so that when your opportunity comes around you can step onto the mat and perform. I am not a preacher, but unless you are a natural-born athlete, you are going to need a good foundation on which to build your wrestling future. That foundation begins with knowing who you are and what you are about to become, a champion. Start now by thinking about this:

How to become the next state wrestling champion.

Accept the fact that your life will change by following our plan.

Parents Must Do Their Part To Lead The Way

Here is a short story about a performance goal or change I believe every parent of a wrestler should seriously look at. After many reviews of this chapter, I thought about leaving the next part out, but was outvoted. Charles decided to include this story because he wanted you to understand how strongly we feel parental commitment must be towards goal setting and guiding your wrestler in the right direction. Whether the following approach is right for you is not the point. What I am getting at will be readily apparent after you read on.

The idea took root one night in April of 1995. It was my son's eighth grade year in junior high school and at that time my wife and I were hearing stories and rumors about a few of his friends running into trouble with drugs and alcohol. Now, I am not a saint by any means, and know that kids will be kids. Quite frankly, I like my beer and wine as much as the next guy but after arriving late to a friends party one Saturday night, I could not help but notice how foolish we adults act after just a few drinks.

All the adults had been drinking for some time and at one point I overheard one of the parents say something like, "Please stay out of trouble son," as his son was off for a night on the town. I thought to myself, what *exactly* does "stay out of trouble" mean? What he actually meant to say was stay away from alcohol.

A proven plan that guarantees success.

In thinking about what he had meant, I also realized how hypocritical he and all of us who were sending our children the same message were being. How can parents tell their children to stay out of trouble and away from alcohol when we parents abuse it and look stupid at the same time? It simply does not equate.

That night I decided not to drink. In the morning I called Charles into my room and told him that I had made an even bigger decision than to simply not drink alcohol on that one particular night. I had decided not to have another drink of alcohol until he graduated from high school. I would not have another drink, cold turkey, for the next four years.

I realize that we all make our share of mistakes in life and that I am in no position to tell you what you need to do with your life. I am simply trying to show through my decision that you can make a commitment in life and stick to it if you believe you can.

I had been telling Charles about the importance of change in his life. I knew that although leading by example was going to be tough, it was necessary for both of us. This was a major step towards developing trust between the two of us. He was making some big sacrifices to reach his goals in life and I felt that it was necessary to help him by leading the way.

Charles graduated high school in June of 1998 and I did not have a single drop of alcohol until some time after graduation day. I stuck to my commitment, and actually, together we both stuck to our guns.

Your Pathway To Success

By reading this book, you will learn how to get on a winning path and stay there. You will also get an understanding of how to approach the sport and why Charles and I know this approach works. You will learn that wrestling is bigger than winning and losing. It is a journey your whole family can learn from and this book will make sure you pack only the essentials needed for you to get the most out of your experience.

When you go on vacation I am sure you take along a road map to help guide you along the way. The map is essential, which is exactly the reason why you are reading this introduction right now.

Please understand that the road you must take to become a **state champion** is a very tough one. One with a lot of bumps and wrong turns that you might not be prepared for along the way. It is our intention to point out the pitfalls and help you plan your journey around these bumps in the road.

The top of the mountain in our opinion is nothing less than becoming a **state champion**. I have met quite a few coaches over the last few years that were never able to fulfill their dream of becoming a **state champion**. Each one of them would gladly go back and start over if they could and use this guide as their road map to achieving wrestling success.

By obtaining a copy of this plan you have already taken the all-important first step of separating yourself from the crowd. You have acknowledged that you want more for yourself than the average wrestler wants for themselves. As you progress through each chapter, imagine

A proven plan that guarantees success.

that we are right there with you. Although this is our story and plan, it will soon become yours as well. Everyone that loves the sport of wrestling will get something out of this book.

Hopefully by now you are starting to understand the essence of the book's message, which is:

ENJOY YOUR WRESTLING JOURNEY BECAUSE IT IS ONLY GOING TO LAST FOR A BRIEF PERIOD OF YOUR LIFE. ALTHOUGH IT IS JUST A PART OF YOUR DEVELOPMENT AS A PERSON, IT CAN BE THE KEY THAT OPENS THE DOOR TO A VERY BRIGHT FUTURE.

Step One

Working Smart

What Is Working Smart?

"Without a Working Smart plan you are planning to fail."
- The Martelli's

Hard work is a term many people use when referring to the sport of wrestling. We are here to put into perspective the trying tasks of lifting weights, drilling, and hard wrestling through our developed training philosophy: **Working Smart**. Learning what **Working Smart** involves and implementing it into your workout habits is essential to becoming a **state champion**.

Young wrestlers, including you, may read articles in various wrestling publications about the ways wrestlers have worked hard to win their state titles. These articles tell the tale of long,

A proven plan that guarantees success.

grueling workouts. They tell of the endless hours of sweat pouring and weight cutting these wrestlers have gone through. They may even include anecdotes on all the adversities the wrestlers had to overcome while working through problems involving diet or injury.

We have discovered that this type of endless, boring, exhaustive training is not always necessary. My father and I knew that there must be a better way to approach training and play catch up. Within these pages we have put together what we have learned from the sport and have laid out our philosophy in the six essential strategies about to follow. If you have the discipline to follow our guidance by reading, reviewing, and putting our **Working Smart** habits into action, winning a state title, or several, will feel as good to you as it did to us.

As you progress through this book you will soon learn that the philosophy of **Working Smart** includes hard work, but encompasses much more than hard work alone. You need to spend time working on fine-tuning the training habits that are going to make you not only a better wrestler but also a better student and person as well.

Do not misunderstand this part of the message by thinking that this book is supposed to be about wrestling and not a lesson in academics. To become a **state champion** you need to excel in all facets of life. If you are wasting your time and having to cram for a test, or focusing your energies on getting into trouble, you will not have the essential time needed to develop the habits of our **Working Smart** philosophy.

Having more time to concentrate on wrestling will reduce the amount of time you will need to play catch-up with those athletes ahead of you. Basically, being responsible inside and outside of the wrestling room is vital to becoming a **state champion**.

How to Begin Working Smart

There are a few things that have to be understood immediately to learn the ins and outs of **Working Smart**. Once you become familiar with them, the journey ahead of you will become much easier. They are the basic building blocks that you cannot skip. You must take these building blocks seriously. Do not overlook any of the steps if you want to be on top of the podium. I have also pointed out some very important words and concepts you will need to adopt to develop a fuller understanding of who you are and what the sport of wrestling is all about.

Start the **Working Smart** philosophy by keeping a journal (notebook) and recording what it is you did during each of your workouts. Keeping a well-organized journal will prove to be an extremely valuable tool on your path to victory. One of the things that I have learned on my journey is the true value of writing everything down. Do not let valuable information go to waste by not writing it down. Get a notebook today and start writing.

Having a good system of note-taking will allow you to look back and see what you have done and what you have not done in terms of workouts. You will be able to skim through pages of technique to catch the one fine point you forgot on a double leg finish. Remembering the little things is a key to success. One day the little things might be the difference between getting to

A proven plan that guarantees success.

the top of the podium and being on the end of the podium.

Although obvious and basic to some, the concepts of passion, bravery, fear, procrastination, hard-work, and the fact that there are no shortcuts in wrestling need to be addressed so that you can truly understand and feel what we are teaching you. These building blocks are part of the foundation that makes up our thrilling sport of wrestling.

Develop Passion: Have a burning desire. It is a flame that burns deep within you. It is a love for whatever it is you choose to do and doing it to the best of your ability. It is impossible to survive all of the ups and downs and bumps and bruises that wrestling dishes out without a passion for the sport. If you have a passion for the sport, and I know you do since you are reading this book, it will automatically challenge you to push for the next level.

Discover Bravery: If you have ever seen or heard of the movie *Braveheart* you will not have to look up the word "brave" in Webster's Dictionary. You already have a clear understanding of its meaning. For those of you who are not familiar with the film, make sure you rent it and watch it. For now, I will give you a quick lesson on what it means to be brave.

Bravery is about having courage—the mental capacity and strength to stand strong no matter what the odds are. It is about becoming fearless, bold, and daring regardless of what danger lies ahead of you. Bravery is being able shake your opponent's hand firmly, no matter how much better or worse he is than you, and then attack relentlessly for six minutes, and not back down for one fraction of a second until the final whistle is blown.

"Courage is like a muscle; it is strengthened by use."
- *Ruth Gordon*

Overcome Fear: How many times have you thought the worst about a scenario and the worst never happened the way you imagined it? Fear is simply a figment of your imagination. To handle and conquer fear you need to recognize it, get in touch with it, and realize that it is not real. It is simply made up in your mind. The best way to handle fear is to understand why there is fear and then to replace the fear with good, old-fashioned smart work in the practice room.

Through smart work you will develop a self-confidence that will wash out the conjured up fear in your mind. You will know you have worked harder than your opponents, and that you are going to win. Do not confuse nervousness with fear. It is almost guaranteed that you will get butterflies before every match (everyone does before going into battle), but fear is something that can be defeated with smart work. Once again, it only exists in your mind and can be beaten, just like your opponent can.

Beat Procrastination: If you are like most people you probably have those days when you just do not want to get out of bed. It would be much easier to hit the snooze button for ten more minutes than to tackle the day's chores that lie ahead. You most likely even have days where you

A proven plan that guarantees success.

would love to spend an extra hour at the pool with your friends rather than to get your wrestling workout in.

A pure definition of procrastination is putting off what absolutely needs to be done. For instance, it is replacing your workouts with tasks that are easier and unnecessary. You need to come to the realization, as we have, that you must take action and get to your workouts despite all the circumstances. Do not let what your body is telling you get in the way of becoming a **state champion** wrestler. You must be strong when your body is ordering you to sleep just a little while longer or to watch one more television program.

Know that every once in a while when you feel lazy, your competition may be feeling the same way. For your sake, imagine your opponents staying in bed those ten extra minutes, leaving the door wide open for you to catch up or sail ahead of them. These days give you incentive to train smarter. When you know that your competition is not getting up at six in the morning to lift, you are giving yourself an extra incentive to get up early. You will soon realize that these days occur more frequently than you think and can add up quickly, providing you with added gain.

Also, understand that everyone needs a little help sometimes. Do not be afraid to ask your support team (friends, family, coaches, and teammates) for a little push. If you take full advantage of the times your opponents are doing nothing, you will soon realize how quickly you can move toward your goal of winning a state title.

There Is No Substitute For Hard Work: This statement is bottom line. There is no substitute for hard work. There is no substitute for hard work. No, this is not a typo. This phrase is repeated for a specific reason. You must take this to heart and think it through carefully. You cannot go to the athletic store and say to the store clerk, "Hello. Where can I buy two pounds of muscle?" or "Where can I find an extra pair of lungs? I have been getting winded during practice lately.". To think this is absurd.

The only way to add two pounds of muscle to your frame or ten minutes to your conditioning level is through smart, hard work. Pushing your conditioning wall back each and every practice will allow you to wrestle harder and longer. You will be able to break your opponent's mental toughness that much easier. Nothing negative comes out of hard work and you cannot lose anything by doing it. Conversely, without hard work there is the potential to lose everything—including your state title.

"I think good physical conditioning is essential to any occupation. A man who is physically fit performs better at any job. Fatigue makes cowards of us all."
- Vincent Lombardi

There Are No Easy Ways Out or Shortcuts: This concept is just as important to comprehend as the one above and is rather self-explanatory. The easy way out is a shortcut and a shortcut is the easy way out. Taking the easy way out by not working hard or procrastinating will only spell

A proven plan that guarantees success.

DISASTER. It is that simple. Shortcuts lead to a dead end street, not the top of the podium. Champions do not cut corners, champions seek out challenges. Champions understand hard work and that nowhere in the definition of hard work does the word *easy* or *short* come into play. Enough said!!!

The Beginning

Now that you have begun building your foundation in understanding the terms and concepts above, it is time to start working on the specific areas that make up your plan of attack. Below is a list of **Working Smart** habits that you need to review on a weekly basis. They are a list of checks and balances that will challenge you to think and keep you on the path to success. You may have some of your own personal ideas or habits to add to the list, which is great. However, it is most important that you review these habits weekly and follow through by reviewing your actions religiously with a coach, parent, or drill partner.

- Attain high levels of intensity throughout your wrestling workouts
- Maximize your gains in the weight room
- Balance your aerobic and anaerobic training
- Upgrade your workout partners frequently
- Develop an aggressive attacking style
- Set daily goals
- Remember to ask yourself, "Did I get better today?"

How to become the next state wrestling champion.

- Do something for your sport everyday (364 days a year)
- Vary your workout routines
- Learn how to handle setbacks
- Begin each workout with a proper warm-up
- Understand: being around better people makes you better

Many of these habits are self-explanatory, but remember, you need to review each of these weekly. It is a good idea to put this list on the inside cover of your note-taking tablet for quick reference. This way you will be able to keep special tabs on your daily progress and measure your improvements. You will also be able to weed out any bad habits you may have previously acquired. Here are a few beneficial habits in need of particular attention:

Intensity: One particular college coach that was interested in recruiting me after my first state title mentioned to my father that he liked the intensity I put into my workouts. My dad knew that this coach had only seen me work out a few times, so he asked how he was able to single me out when there were sixty wrestlers out on the mat during this one practice session. His answer was short and simple: Sweat. More specifically, he responded, "The only spot on the mat with sweat all over it was where Chuck was working out."

The point of this little story is that *coaches notice all*. Whether you are drilling or lifting weights, do not waste your time if you are not going to put intensity into the work- out. You will not improve in strength, conditioning, or technique if you do not have intensity in your workouts each and every day.

A proven plan that guarantees success.

Workout Partners: I will cover this topic in greater detail later but you must know that you are only going to be as good as your best workout partner. If you are not working out with someone of **state champion** caliber you are going to have trouble becoming a **state champion**.

Managing Your Time: Write out a time line to map out a plan of attack that specifies where you want to be and when you want to be there. My dad and I realized early that catching up with my competition was essential to winning.

Most of the competitors I encountered had been wrestling since they were four or five years old. I did not start until I was twelve years old, which gave my competition a six- or seven-year advantage. If you got into the sport of wrestling late, as I did, there is a good chance you have fallen slightly behind. Do not worry. You will be able to catch up and move past them! This not only means catch-up in terms of wrestling but also through strength, conditioning, and overall knowledge of the sport.

A good time line with a clear, precise plan of attack will prove to be important. "When in doubt write it out." Your plan should include both monthly and yearly details of where you want to see yourself. We hope that it is on top of the podium wearing the gold medal!

Daily Goals: This topic will be a recurring theme throughout this book, but I would like to point out one detail: There are thousands of books written that stress the importance of goals and goal setting. This must mean that goals are an important aspect of life and should be integrated into your development as a wrestler. If you set up a good time line for your progress it will include

How to become the next state wrestling champion.

your long-range goals. To begin your time line, you must have a daily technique goal and a daily performance goal set before every practice. By doing this as part of your daily preparation your mental focus will become strong and allow for maximum physical gain.

364 Days A Year In Training: Do something for your sport everyday. There will be days when you cannot work out due to prior obligations or injury, but this does not mean that you cannot move closer to your state title. When you cannot work out, or need a supplemental workout, there are numerous options such as:

- Reviewing wrestling film
- Reading about wrestling
- Sending out letters to coaches with questions on a particular technique
- Attending a meet in the area in which you are not competing in to scout competition

Bruce Jenner, a Decathlon Champion and Olympic Gold Medal Winner, adopted this habit and succeeded immensely with it. Bruce's first time at the Olympic games was a huge disappointment. He fell short of his goals and finished out of medal contention. After this finish he decided to alter his time line and daily goal setting habits. He dedicated himself to another four years of training, determined to reach his dream of becoming an Olympic Gold Medalist. Part of his plan included training 364 days of the year, with December 25th as his only day of rest. Bruce Jenner's relentless pursuit of excellence combined with a structured training program won him his childhood dream: An Olympic Gold Medal.

A proven plan that guarantees success.

Setbacks: Along your journey toward becoming a **state champion** there are going to be some temporary setbacks. You must be prepared for these. When you encounter set- backs you must:

- Regain focus and realign your thinking to recognize the good that can be learned from these negative situations.
- Do not allow yourself to get caught up in the "woulda, shoulda, coulda" of what happened.
- Search out your weak links, or as Dan Gable would say, "lesser strengths," and strengthen them immediately.
- Set new goals, both long and short term
- Re-evaluate your goals continuously throughout your progression

SPECIAL NOTE TO PARENTS: For every negative comment you make to your wrestler, you must tell them one hundred positive, reinforcing comments to maintain a proactive working atmosphere. The bottom line is, think positive before you speak because a verbal setback can be just as detrimental as a physical setback.

For you wrestlers out there, avoid excuses. Coaches and teammates do not care about excuses, but they do care that you learn from your setbacks and make the adjustments that will facilitate improvements.

Surround Yourself With Better People: It is essential that you do not waste time surrounding yourself with time-wasters. Avoid those teammates who irritate coaches and fans because they misuse all of their time trying to "look busy or fake injury." In reality, it takes just as much effort, if not more, to pretend to be busy than to accomplish the task at hand.

Seek out friends and workout partners that have the same aspirations and goals as you do. If you surround yourself with people who want to work smart to become a **state champion** then your chances of becoming a **state champion** will increase exponentially. Do not let time-wasters and "slackers" get in the way of achieving your goals.

You cannot go back and retrieve the minutes lost while doing nothing. There are only 24 hours in a day, not a single second more, which means that there is no such thing as "extra time." No matter how you look at it, you only get 1,440 minutes during the day to accomplish your daily goals. Make the most of the present and look forward to utilizing the future.

The philosophy of **Working Smart** is easy. If you are dedicated to developing the proper habits that I have outlined, understand it will take a lot of discipline and time to perfect them. This especially holds true if you adhere to the **Working Smart** message that calls for a review of your workout habits on a weekly basis. However, do not be alarmed if you happen to review one habit more than the rest on one particular week. Some weeks you will be more focused on one habit than the others. This is fine as long as you are working equally, on average, on all the habits I mentioned.

Remember to always think of new and creative ways to improve your habits. Look at your training from an outsider's perspective and ask yourself, "If that were my teammate training, what would I do differently to improve his workout habits?" Taking a good look at yourself from outside your internal box is a helpful technique to pinpoint flaws you might otherwise overlook.

Within the contexts of the **Working Smart** habits there are some very specific ideas that must be incorporated to start formulating your own **Working Smart** plan. The next few chapters will give you a better understanding of the specifics needed to put your own personal plan into action. As you can see, **Working Smart** is the foundation on which you must build your plan for becoming a **state champion** wrestler.

Keep this next quote in mind when you evaluate how you approach your current workouts:

"Without a Working Smart plan, you are planning to fail."
- The Martelli's

Chapter Summary

1. You must have discipline to make the **Working Smart** philosophy work.
2. You not only have to work to become a better wrestler, but a better person and student as well.
3. Keep detailed notes of your workouts in a journal.
4. Know what it means to have passion, be brave, control fear, avoid procrastination, work hard, and eliminate shortcuts.

How to become the next state wrestling champion.

5. Review the following **Working Smart** habits weekly with a coach, family member, or drill partner:
   - Intensity
   - Finding challenging workout partners
   - Time management
   - Set daily goals and attack them 364 days a year
   - Be aware of potential setbacks
   - Surround yourself with proactive people

A proven plan that guarantees success.

Step Two

One-On-One
Not Two-On-One

More Practice Partners *Does Not* Mean Better Practice

"If you keep doing what you've always done you'll keep getting what you've always got."
- *Peter Francisco*

The more you work with better people, coaches, and wrestling partners, the better wrestler you are going to become. It is 100% essential that you seek out **One-on-One** instruction from coaches who have far superior wrestling skills than you if you want to become a **state champion**. It is a simple fact that with better coaching you will become a better wrestler. It is something that all wrestlers think about from time to time but fail to utilize on a regular basis.

A proven plan that guarantees success.

For you to understand the **One-on-One** principle it is essential that you start taking the concept of *individualized coaching* very seriously. Take an immediate evaluation of your wrestling activities and the speed at which your wrestling is progressing.

Remember earlier when I said that for things in your life to change you are going to have to change? Well, this is the perfect starting point. There is no better time than the present. Read this next comment very closely and take it to heart, it may be the most powerful message in this book: **THE ONE-ON-ONE PRINCIPLE WILL PROVIDE YOU WITH THE SINGLE MOST IMPORTANT TOOL TO AID YOUR WRESTLING CAREER**. You will begin to understand the significance of this principle as I lay it out on the following pages.

Getting Started with One-on-One

Training with champions makes champions. Working with better wrestling partners makes better wrestlers. This is plain, simple and factual. But how many people put these well-known facts into action for themselves? Let alone on a daily basis? Even though these are proven facts, my dad and I did not realize how significant this part of the training process was to success. To illustrate that working with people who are better will only make you better I would like to give a training scenario from my own experience.

During the first three years of my wrestling career I wrestled for the same club, both folkstyle and freestyle. During the summer months, when

How to become the next state wrestling champion.

local freestyle competition was long over, I attended various camps in search of the extra edge I knew I needed to beat my competition. While I felt that attending numerous summer camps was the best method for getting ahead, due to my lack of wrestling experience, it was not the type of training I was going to need to become a **state champion**. I needed to seek out a coach with the best credentials I could find to give me **One-on-One** instruction.

The search for a coach for my **One-on-One** training began with my dad speaking with other wrestling coaches and parents around our area. He knew that there might be several high school coaches with prior high school wrestling experience that could offer some of their time to help me, but felt that I needed someone with college wrestling experience. Someone with a college wrestling background would be able to push me past the competition I was seeing every week. Through word of mouth and a little phone book research my dad was able to find me **One-on-One** coaching with an experienced college wrestler. This coach's college background gave me the knowledge and experience I needed to win two state titles.

If you are going to succeed in this sport, and I know you will, it is important to realize that even though you wrestle on a team or for a club, wrestling is ultimately an individual sport! This is where the evaluation of your wrestling progress comes into play.

To find good **One-on-One** instruction you are going to have to spend time doing some research. This could include word of mouth research, as my dad did for me, or other methods such as:

A proven plan that guarantees success.

- Explore high school or college websites for a list of names to contact.
- Go to a nearby college program and talk to wrestlers or coaches personally about **One-on-One** help.
- Read through wrestling publications to find a name, phone number, or face of someone familiar with college experience that you never realized lived in your area.

Regardless of the research method you and your parents may use to find your **One- on-One** coaching, it is crucial that you find the best environment to suit your individual wrestling needs. It is very easy for athletes to get into ruts by settling into a comfortable, moderate training program. Many wrestlers stay in the same club year after year drilling and sparring with the same partners every practice.

Do not get me wrong, there is nothing wrong with wrestling with the same club each year as long as you make sure you are getting variety in your workouts. You should avoid seeking out your buddies who are comfortable to wrestle and drill with every practice. If you do not change your practice partner frequently you will become stagnant.

It is very hard for some of us to put change into motion, especially when things are comfortable, so pay attention to these two very important points. They will aid you throughout the change process:

For your wrestling to change, you are going to have to change: You cannot control the bad training habits of others. To get moving in the right direction toward permanent change, you need to concentrate on implementing our **One-on-**

One principle. You must begin working on the building blocks and habits we outlined in the chapter titled **Working Smart**.

Variety is the spice of life: Once you decide to start making changes, consider some of the following simple ideas to help prevent redundancy in your training. Put variety in your weightlifting, change wrestling partners as often as possible, work out at different times throughout the day, bike or swim instead of running, or perfect a new set-up. Spicing up workouts with variety in several of the areas mentioned will prevent you from getting burned out or bored.

Follow My Lead

If you do not remember anything else from what you read, please remember what is laid out in the rest of this chapter. Try to integrate my firsthand experiences with the sport of wrestling into your routines and daily practices.

Becoming a great folkstyle and freestyle wrestler was simply not enough for me. Having the chance to win a state title was not enough either. I was out for multiple state titles and much more. I wanted the pie in the sky and the glory that came with it. With this desire for success, my dad and I accepted the challenge to make me a champion.

During the spring and summer before entering high school I decided to change wrestling clubs for the first time. I have to admit I was nervous at first. I had been with the same coach and teammates for three years and had gotten comfortable with my training tactics. (As I mentioned, this happens with many young wrestlers). My father assured me that this change was necessary if I wanted to be the best, which I did.

My dad heard that a young coach with great credentials was starting a club about thirty miles from where we lived. Coach Dan Knight was a four-time Iowa **state champion** and had won multiple cadet and junior national titles, to name a few of his amazing accomplishments. Although we knew that the move would cause both transportation and time conflicts we decided to switch clubs anyway. After all, if things were not working out I could always return to the old club and continue my search for better training. In my dad's and my eyes, there was no downside to the change. The upside was that working with a coach that was exceptionally better than me would only make me better. What more could I have asked for?

Taking Out An Assurance Policy

The first step towards me becoming a two-time **state champion** was not only changing coaching and clubs, it was realizing that I had to be provided with some type of **Assurance Policy**. I am sure you have heard of an insurance policy before and understand what it entails. However, do not get an insurance policy confused with an **Assurance Policy**. An insurance policy guarantees protection against certain types of losses. On the other hand, an **Assurance Policy** (**One-on-One** instruction) provides confidence and surety that a task can be completed. For me to become a **state champion** I needed confidence

How to become the next state wrestling champion.

and surety. A wrestling **Assurance Policy** helped prevent obstacles from getting in the way of me winning state titles. It gave me the confidence and sureness that nothing would prevent me from winning.

The initial lack of organization at my new club left my dad and I unimpressed. I was used to the same structured warm-up, the same structured drill, and the same structured live wrestling every practice. It was an extremely mechanical practice sprinkled with minute variations. While the new club's system may have been different from the old, we soon noticed a real benefit in the way Coach Knight presented his technique, what he was teaching, and how he handled himself on and off the mat. He was one person who was **Working Smart**.

Dan Knight soon became a great role model for me to emulate and follow. Finally, I had found a home where a true champion was training future champions. I could not ask for a better opportunity. The team practiced twice a week, but to get the **Assurance Policy** I had been looking for, I felt I needed to find out if Coach Knight would work **One-on-One** with me. Approaching Coach Knight about the idea of working **One-on-One** could not have been easier. He reacted with an energetic "yes." So my dad and I made the sixty-mile round trip once a week, and even twice a week on several occasions, to get the **One-on-One** help I needed.

Asking a coach to work **One-on-One** with you might seem difficult and intimidating. However, you have nothing to fear. Most coaches are pleasantly surprised to learn that there is someone impressed enough with their wrestling skills to ask them for personal help. Here are

A proven plan that guarantees success.

some good tips on appropriate ways to approach a coach for **One-on-One** help:

- Talk with a coach after a practice
- Do not be afraid to ask for their phone numbers and call them at work or at home. They will welcome your interest.
- Be polite, courteous, and sincere about your interest in their help.
- Tell the coach why you are seeking their help.
- Write down the dates and times they are available.
- Coordinate **One-on-One** coaching sessions from the list of dates you have recorded.
- Make sure to offer them compensation for their time and effort that is fair for both of you.
- Plan your first session and discover how quickly you will improve your wrestling skills.

Coach Knight kept a close watch over me and often gave me extra attention when practice was over. After observing my intensity and enthusiasm during practice he knew I had the desire to move ahead and become a **state champion**. Coach Knight knew I was a smart worker. This made him willing to sacrifice some of his personal time to help me. Coach Knight's unselfish attitude helped me progress from an average freestyle wrestler to one of the best Cadet wrestlers in the state.

During my first high school season I finished with a 26-6 record earning my first varsity letter and establishing myself as an athlete to watch. I had the will to succeed, the passion to train, and an unyielding desire to

How to become the next state wrestling champion.

achieve my goal of winning multiple state titles. **One-on-One** instruction in the off season with a coach and partners who were much better than me proved to be the single best **Assurance Policy** to give me the confidence and surety needed to get to the next level.

In the spring following my freshman year I decided to look for more help in terms of a good **One-on-One** wrestling partner. I needed another partner with college wrestling experience that could be a first-class role model, and at the same time provide more frequent intense **One-on-One** wrestling closer to home.

One afternoon, in 1996, at the local hardware store my dad started up a conversation with a young man that looked to be an experienced wrestler. His cauliflower ear was a clear sign he had been in a match or two over the years. They talked for nearly an hour and as luck would have it, the man, Tom Champion, turned out to be the person I was looking for.

It was almost destiny that my dad walked into the hardware store that day. Tom turned out to be not only one of my best friends over the years but he was also one of the most worthwhile **Assurance Policies** I could have gotten. We hit it off immediately. Tom had a unique ability to work at my level, despite the fact that he was almost ten years my elder. Tom had a knack for always staying a few steps ahead of me to ensure steady progress. Slowly but surely Tom was pushing me up towards the level I needed to get to. His college experiences and love for the sport were two key ingredients that enhanced the productivity of my training.

While working with Tom as frequently as possible, I still made occasional trips in the summer to work with Coach Knight, but only to

A proven plan that guarantees success.

participate in regular club practices. Unfortunately, a few of the high school parents did not like the fact that Coach Knight was helping a wrestler from another school. I had to keep it low-key and cut out most of the **One-on-One** instruction I had previously been receiving. I am very grateful to Coach Dan Knight, who now coaches at Mount St. Claire College in Clinton, Iowa. I suggest you look him up if you are around that area and model his **Working Smart** tactics.

Tom Champion continued to work with other wrestlers and myself by volunteering his time in my high school wrestling room. He is still there pumping out one champion after another. In fact, we still workout together and have great fun doing so.

My sophomore year, the same year I started to work with Coach Champion, the **One-on-One** concept really paid off. I took third place in the state at 145 lbs. My only loss during the state tournament was to a four-time Illinois **state champion**. I won conference, the Regional tournament, pinned everyone in the Sectional tournament, and finished, wearing a third place medal at the state tournament. Also, I set my high school record for takedowns that year.

It is imperative to realize what the results can be if you follow the **One-on-One** principle of personal coaching. Learn from people who are much better than you. If you begin to believe in this approach to training you can have the same results that I had. Make a move and invest in an **Assurance Policy** that will guarantee you confidence, victory, and success. Hopefully you can see the value that a **One-on-One Assurance Policy** will have on your wresting career.

How to become the next state wrestling champion.

> "The minute you start talking about what you're going to do if you lose, you have lost."
> - *George Shultz*

Chapter Summary

1. **One-on-One training with the best coaching you can find is the single most important change you will make for your wrestling career.**
2. Evaluate your wrestling progress regularly.
3. Working out with better people will only make you better.
4. Although you wrestle on a team, wrestling is ultimately an individual sport.
5. Seek out the best wrestling environment in your area.
6. For things to change for you, you are going to have to change.
7. Variety is the spice of life.
8. Take out a **One-on-One Assurance Policy** for your wrestling.

A proven plan that guarantees success.

Step Three

Adopt A Winning Wrestling Style

Adopt a Winning Style

If you can fully understand the following three points of adopting a winning wrestling style, you will be well on your way to dominating your competition.

- When you are on the mat, you are in your own world. You have the ability to be anyone you want to be. Why not be the best, the toughest, and the meanest? To succeed in wrestling you need to have a mean streak. Turn yourself into an animal and make the mat your domain. Anyone who steps into your domain will have to answer to the animal inside you and suffer the consequences for intruding on your territory.
- The opponent standing across the mat from you wants to take away everything you have worked for and make it his own. He wants to crush your dreams of becoming a

high school **state champion**, destroy your pride, and take all of your smart, hard work away by pinning both of your shoulders to the mat. He wants to win. Do not let him!
- Your mindset has to be ATTACK, ATTACK, ATTACK, one hundred percent of the time. You must be relentless in your pursuit of victory. Search and destroy whoever steps onto your territory. Pin your opponent before he pins you.

Once you are able to understand each of these points, you will be able to adopt a physical and brawling wrestling style in which you will crush your competition. You must realize that you own every inch of the wrestling mat from the moment you step on it. Your opponents want to beat you by any means necessary and you cannot stop attacking them at any cost.

In one of my favorite movies about World War II, titled *Patton*, there is an excellent quote from one particular scene that encompasses all three of the above points.

While on the phone with military personnel, General Patton, a four-star general (next to the highest rank attainable in the army), tells his subordinates that he will not stop his troops from attacking. His advisors want him to be conservative, slow down, hold back, and to become defensive; after all, war is not something to play around with. General Patton is extremely annoyed at these requests and in a very loud, assertive tone he responds forcefully with the following quote:

"We are going to attack all night and all morning. If we are not victorious let no man come back alive."
- *General George S. Patton, Jr.*

Resting, holding back, becoming defensive, pacing yourself, and being cautious are for your opponent. To become a high school **state champion** you must be ferocious with a style that is constructed from the following wrestling characteristics:

- Brawling
- Pushing
- Shoving
- Snapping
- Faking
- Intimidating
- Attacking
- Dominating
- Pinning

Rid yourself of the following characteristics that guarantee failure:

- Fear
- Defensiveness
- Stalling
- Laziness
- Reservation

You must learn to develop an aggressive offense that your competition is afraid of. Your opponents should be afraid to step on the mat because they know you will attack relentlessly

until your hand has been raised in victory. You must be offensive and attack every second of the match. **DO NOT STOP OR RETREAT AT ANY POINT.**
In the words of NCAA Division I National Champion Terry Steiner, "If you are on the offense the entire match, nothing bad can happen to you." I cannot emphasize this point enough. The more you are attacking your opponent the less time he has to attack you. This translates to points being scored, victories being tallied, and state titles being won.

Attitude

To adopt a winning wrestling style you need to be full of "attitude." You must stride onto the mat energized by both anger and motivation for victory. You must hate that your opponent wants to physically beat you and embarrass you. Your confidence level should border on arrogance.
Although you must be confident and fearless, **NEVER BE A POOR SPORT**. No matter how big of an attitude you carry with you to the mat or how confident you are, as soon as you step off the mat you must revert to your gentlemanly self. Along with a fearless, mean attitude comes the responsibility of conducting yourself with class and self-respect off the mat.
When I was in high school my teammates gave me the nickname "the animal." Although this nickname sounded crazy, I accepted it with pride. However, once I was off the mat and out of the practice room I made sure to transform back to my normal, calm self. The fact that my teammates were calling me "the animal" gave me

the confidence I needed to believe that; if my teammates thought I had the attitude of a caged animal and that I wrestled to destroy my competition, then my opponents must have been extremely intimidated to wrestle me. Your opponents must fear stepping on the mat with you in the same manner as mine did.

This is the type of nickname you want to earn from your wrestling style and attitude on the mat. You want your opponents to know that you mean nothing but business once you step your foot on the line and shake hands. Develop an attitude that creates fear and intimidation in the mind of your competition. This will give you a huge mental edge before the whistle even blows.

The Essence Of Attitude

Just before the state tournament my junior year of high school I was interviewed by a local newspaper about how I was going to complete my currently undefeated season and win my first state title. The following day the article was published in the paper with an answer to that question. It read, "I am going to stage a relentless attack."

I was not being arrogant; I was stating a fact. I had great confidence in my attitude and wrestling style. I felt that in order to win the state title of my dreams I needed to have a relentless attack. This straightforward style is what I am preaching to you now.

After years of smart, hard work I had reached the point where I was not going to let anyone step onto *my* territory and take away *my* state title without going through war first. You

A proven plan that guarantees success.

must get yourself to the same point by practicing and implementing your own plan similar to the one laid out in this book. Develop an attitude, adopt a wrestling style that creates fear, and become confident enough to know you will attack relentlessly until you are on top of the podium wearing the gold medal.

"If there was just one word I could use to describe a successful person, that one word would be attitude."
- Bart Starr

The Process of Adopting A Style

Now that I have laid out the groundwork of adopting a wrestling style, I will take you through the process of creating your own winning style. My mindset in high school was that if was is good enough for Dan Gable, the most famous US wrestler in history, it was good enough for me and it certainly will be for you as well.

Gable won every match but one throughout his high school and college career and won an Olympic gold medal without having a single point scored against him. With a style that centers on attitude and unrelenting offense like Gable's, you can win state title after state title with the same style. Why not model yourself after what works? This plan of attack won two high school state titles for me without any prior wrestling experience before entering sixth grade.

To become successful at something you must study it. I decided to sit down and study college-wrestling programs that were successful

How to become the next state wrestling champion.

with a dominating physical style of attack. While developing my style in high school I needed to know what characteristics were making certain individuals and programs consistently successful. **IF IT WORKS AT THE HIGHEST LEVEL IT IS GOING TO WORK AT THE LOWEST LEVEL AND EVERYWHERE IN BETWEEN.**
After figuring out which teams had the most successful style, I did whatever I could to study them. I got videotapes featuring wrestlers dominating their competition. I noticed several reoccurring tactics each wrestler on the tapes embodied and made mental notes of them:

- Always the aggressors
- Very physical with their opponents
- Controlling their opponents
- Always moving forward
- Domination of actual mat space
- Always on the offense
- Scoring on both the edge and middle of the mat
- Mentally tougher than their opponents
- Better conditioned
- Have noticeably mean and confident attitudes

It is tremendously important to recognize two underlying features found in the statements above: Aggression and attitude. Understand and learn that what works for the best at very high levels of competition will also work for you. Being aggressive the entire match and having a nasty attitude on the mat will win you a state title.

Get videotapes of the successful wrestlers you like to watch and who you want to model yourself after. Find people who are winning and dominating their competition. Start adopting their style and attitude. It is highly beneficial to your success in the sport of wrestling to start compiling film of those who are winning. Begin building a library that depicts the wrestling style you want to adopt.

Pick out which characteristics of the wrestlers in your video library that make them successful. I can tell you right now from years of experience in watching film, the winners will always have an aggressive style that is full of attitude. It will be worth your while to invest some time studying film. I guarantee it.

"It's hard to beat a person who never gives up."

- Babe Ruth

Technique For A Winning Style

Once you determine that you want to adopt a winning style of aggressive, relentless wrestling with a mean attitude, there are several technique areas you have to concentrate on. Understand that there are some techniques that will work better than others when state titles are on the line.

Takedowns: There are no magical or secret takedowns that only successful wrestlers use. What they do use is solid technique that has long stood the test of time. You must perfect solid takedown techniques that can be used on any opponent at any time. These include:

- The single leg
- The double leg
- The high crotch
- The front headlock

If you perfect these four offensive takedowns, you cannot go wrong. Each of these takedowns has worked for hundreds of years and has won thousands of **state championships**. Spend your time developing and perfecting these takedowns along with your relentless style of wrestling. They will not betray you.

Controlling your opponent: You must control your opponent at all times. This means that during every second of a match you have to grab onto and control an elbow, a hand, a wrist, the head, the neck, or any combination of these body parts. It is crucial that you are in control of your opponent, and not the other way around. If you are not controlling a part of your opponent, then you are not being relentless and offensive.

The set-up: The most often overlooked aspect of wrestling is the set-up. I cannot emphasize enough how critical a set-up is to winning a state title. If you can adopt a relentless style of wrestling with a physical attitude, set-ups will be easy to perfect. They will develop out of your pushing, shoving, and brawling. The more you push, shove, and brawl with your opponent, the more times they will be forced out of good position and are set up for a great takedown.

Without a set-up there cannot be a takedown. Remember this and practice opening up your opponent by being physical. Create openings for attacks. Keep your opponent off balance at all times. Use the brawling strategy to increase your opportunities for scoring points and winning matches. Adopt a relentless attack and discover that setting up a takedown will take care of itself. The more offensive scoring opportunities you can create through set ups and being physical, the more points you will put on the scoreboard.

The pin: If you want to be an aggressive, mean, and dominant wrestler, you must work to pin every opponent that you wrestle. Pinning in the sport of wrestling is the ultimate feat, which is why they are worth the most team points (six). People attend wrestling matches hoping to see a pin at every weight class. As former University of Michigan wrestler and two-time All-American, Sean Bormet, says, "Pain and pressure equals a pin." He is 100% correct.

You cannot be afraid to inflict pain and pressure on your opponent; both are necessary throughout your hunt for a state title. Adopt a winning style of wrestling that:

- Is aggressive
- Is full of a mean attitude
- Creates pain and pressure while working to dominantly pin your opponent's shoulders to the mat

Creating An Offensive Defense

An offensive defense means that when your opponent attacks offensively, you instantly smother them with your own defensive attacks to score points. Defense is not in your arsenal of techniques simply for fighting off your opponent. It is there to fight off your opponents, stop them from scoring, and turn their bad offensive shots into scoring opportunities of your own.

To develop your offensive defense you must spend hours working on fighting off your opponent's attacks and learning to score off of them. Examples of offensive defenses include:

- Front head locks
- Butt drags
- Short drags
- Beating the arm
- Quarter nelsons
- Gator rolls

Spend time in offensive defensive positions. Master the art of turning a defensive position into a scoring opportunity. To have a winning wresting style with a hunger for scoring points it is essential that you be able to score from every position. If you can develop an offensive defense you will be one step closer to winning a high school state title.

Good luck in finding a few successful wrestlers to model yourself after. As I mentioned earlier, if it works for the best it will work for you. Become relentless and develop an attitude. You will be unstoppable on your mission to a state title with these two characteristics intertwined into your winning wrestling style.

A proven plan that guarantees success.

Chapter Summary

1. When you are on the mat you are the master of your domain. You have the ability to be anyone you want to be.
2. The competitor standing across the mat from you wants to take away everything you have worked for and make it theirs. Do not let them!
3. Your mindset has to be ATTACK, ATTACK, ATTACK, one hundred percent of the time.
4. You have to develop an aggressive offense that your competition is afraid of.
5. "If you are on the offense the entire match nothing bad can happen to you."
6. To adopt a winning wrestling style you need to be full of attitude.
7. Along with a fearless, mean attitude comes the responsibility of conducting yourself with class and self-respect off the mat. Do not forget this, ever!
8. If it works at the highest level it is going to work at the lowest level and everywhere in between. Being aggressive the entire match and having a nasty attitude on the mat will win you a state title.
9. You must obtain some videotapes of wrestlers you like to watch who are successful and will be great models from which to learn.
10. You must perfect solid takedown techniques that can be used on any opponent at any time. These include:
    - The single leg
    - The double leg
    - The high crotch
    - The front headlock

How to become the next state wrestling champion.

11. Control your opponent at all times.
12. If you can adopt a relentless style of wrestling with a physical attitude, set-ups will be easy to perfect.
13. To develop your offensive defense you must spend hours working to fight off your opponent's attacks and learn to score off of them.

A proven plan that guarantees success.

Step Four

Goal Setting

What Is Goal Setting?

"I don't think anything is unrealistic if you believe you can do it. I think if you are determined enough and willing to pay the price, you can get it done."
– Mike Ditka

Goal setting is decision making. By setting a goal you decided that you want to accomplish a task and are willing to do whatever it takes to accomplish that task. Attaining your goal and living your dreams is the main reason we stress **Working Smart**. You must always believe that you can reach what you set out to do. Believing in yourself and your goals is the key to achieving success in wrestling as well as life.

Goals are milestones that line the path on your quest towards greatness. People make goals to keep themselves on a highly motivated track.

A proven plan that guarantees success.

There is no point to wrestling or competing if you do not want to win state titles or be the best. The sport of wrestling is too mean and brutal to be competing in if you are merely hoping to survive. You must strive for greatness.

Goals can be categorized as long-term and short-term, depending upon the time frame in which you are hoping to accomplish specific tasks. Long-term goals can take anywhere from six months to several years to achieve.

Long-term goals are what you are ultimately striving to accomplish. Winning a high school state title would be an example of a long-term goal. To be the best, you must set your long-term goals extremely high. Decide today that you are going to become a high school **state champion**. Set the date you are going to achieve this goal and go do it. Planning out a long-term goal is a helpful way to keep you motivated. Do not be afraid to make the commitment. Without it, you will not be **Working Smart**. You will be lacking a sense of direction, and will be settling for mediocrity. In the sport of wrestling those who compete without direction are easily surpassed by their peers. **YOU MUST DREAM BIG DREAMS!!!**

Short-term goals are stepping stones you set along the way to keep you focused on long-term goals. They are set on a more frequent basis and are not as monumental as long-term goals. Short-term goals can be performance goals. They are set every day, every week, and every month. You should begin each practice with short-term goals. Without pre-set short-term goals integrated into your practices and workouts, you will be stuck "going through the motions." Short-term goals allow you to measure progress, inch by inch, because you have achieved many small accomplishments along the way.

Short-term goals will keep long-term goals within sight while you train to attain them. Setting short-term goals will allow you to see immediate progress during your training, and if needed, will allow you to reevaluate your long-term goals.

It is necessary to have both long and short-term goals because you must be able to measure your improvements. Without goals, it is impossible to remember where you started and where you have progressed in terms of your wrestling ability. You need comparisons to tell you where you have been and where you have the potential to go. Short-term goals will give you the confidence needed to reach your loftier, long-term goals.

Goal setting is a practiced cycle that has proven to be a beneficial tool in the search for individual success. After specific short-term goals are reached, new goals must be set and the step-by-step process begins all over again. Use both long- and short-term goals as motivators and measuring sticks on the way to winning your own high school state title.

Four Crucial Areas Of Short-Term (Performance) Goal Setting

It is crucial that you not only set a goal of becoming a **state champion** wrestler, but that you have other small performance goals along the way. These performance goals are developed to help bring you closer to your dream of winning a state title.

A proven plan that guarantees success.

Performance goals are vital to improving all the facets of wrestling that will win you a state title. Performance goals should be set in each of the following areas:

Anaerobic training: Anaerobic goals are intended to help improve the conditioning of your muscles when they are fatigued and lacking oxygen. Exercises that tear down and rip your muscle fibers and cannot be repeated endlessly are anaerobic.

There are several types of anaerobic conditioning that you can do to help improve this part of your wrestling. They include activities such as:

- Weightlifting
- Pull-ups
- Chin-ups
- Push-ups
- Sit-ups
- Rope climbs
- Manual strength exercises with a partner (strength resistance without weights)

Each of these anaerobic exercises requires you to perform beyond the point where you are completely and utterly exhausted. You muscles should ache and burn painfully, screaming for you to stop using them. The pain and discomfort of tearing down your muscle fibers is what defines anaerobic conditioning.

The one model of anaerobic conditioning that I will use to demonstrate short-term goal setting is weightlifting. Weightlifting is one of the most important anaerobic conditioning areas in the sport of wrestling. It is very important that every time you step into a weight room you have a

How to become the next state wrestling champion.

goal for that particular session. You can set a goal for each weight lifting session in several ways.

- Set a goal depending on the **amount of repetitions** you want to do.
- Set a goal for the **number of sets** you want to do for an exercise or group of exercises.
- Set a goal for the **amount of weight** you want to lift or the amount of weight you want to increase to over a period of time.
- Set these goals for **one day, one week, and several months** of weightlifting sessions.

These are just a few of the types of goals that can be set for weightlifting. Use this model of setting short-term weightlifting goals for all of your anaerobic conditioning activities.

Aerobic training: Aerobic activities are those that condition the heart and body by increasing how well the body takes in and processes oxygen. In the sport of wrestling it is imperative that your body is able to process oxygen very efficiently. Good aerobic conditioning will allow you to wrestle at your peak level for a long period of time, enabling you to physically outlast your opponent. Make your competitor struggle for air.

Aerobic activities will help improve your body's oxygen processing. These activities should be done at a steady pace with a heart rate between 60-90% of your maximum heart rate for at least twenty minutes a session. You can calculate your aerobic heart rate range by subtracting your age in years from 220 and multiplying that number by both .60 and .90

[(220-AGE) X .60 and (220-AGE) X .90]

Exercise such as long distance running, biking, or jumping rope steadily are forms of aerobic training. Setting performance goals for an aerobic activity is rather simple because aerobic activities are measured in one of two ways: *time* or *distance*.

Examples of short-term aerobic goals might include increasing your long distance runs by one tenth of a mile every time you exercise. The next time you bike ride, try and go a little further than the previous time you rode. You might also think about decreasing your times on mapped out distance routes. Work to improve your times by ten seconds in one week or one month. Understand that these are only four examples of what you might want to do when setting short-term aerobic goals. There are dozens of different ways to mix and match your times and distances.

A long-term running goal would be to increase the distance you run, from one mile to several miles (e.g., 5-10) over a six-month period. On the contrary, short-term aerobic goals focus on increasing your distance by one hundred yards each time you run a specific route. You will find that once you start reaching your short-term aerobic goals, your wrestling will improve drastically because your conditioning base will be at a significantly higher level.

Weight Control/Diet: Most people know that wrestling often calls for weight cutting or dieting. Most of the time these steps are hard to avoid unless you are that extremely rare wrestler who can compete successfully in several weight classes.

For most people though, performing at their optimal level with optimal strength requires them to cut to the lowest weight class within their

How to become the next state wrestling champion.

natural weight. There are numerous harmful ways in which many wrestlers cut weight that I will not discuss. Instead, I recommend you focus on healthy means of maintaining your target weight.

Setting goals for dieting is incredibly important. Make sure that you are losing weight in a healthy manner. I will not give specifics on the goals you need to set for weight control because they will vary from one wrestler to the next. However, if you are considering losing weight to move to a lower weight class, I will suggest talking with your parents, coach, family physician and/or a nutritionist to make sure you diet in an appropriate and healthy way.

Drilling/Specific technique: I will discuss drilling more thoroughly later on, so I will not say much on this except that you must have performance goals geared towards improving your technique. Goals that are set for every practice work the best when you are trying to improve a specific technique. For example, you might want to work on perfecting a high crotch takedown that you were never able to finish. Your performance goal for practice could be, "to perfect a high crotch to a double leg finish that no opponent can stop." This could be accomplished over the course of many seasons, one practice at a time, by repeatedly drilling it thirty to forty times a session. You can plug in any technique you wish to perfect into this example. However, it must be done consistently and correctly every time you drill it to make it unbeatable.

Evaluate your technique goals frequently and have either a parent or a coach critique your progress. You cannot win a state title without great technique. You may want to videotape yourself drilling and review the tape later to correct the finer technique points that you would otherwise have missed.

To beat the best you have to out-prepare the best and also outsmart the best. Set plenty of technique and drilling goals, and have the best technique when it counts—in the state finals.

What Do I Do With My Goals?

Once you have committed to what you want to accomplish, you must tell someone your goals and write them down on paper. By doing so you are making a pubic commitment and your goals become more of a reality. Do not skip either of these steps in your goal-setting process.

It is critical that you tell someone what your goals are because it forces you to commit to your words. If you keep your goals hidden inside of your head without anyone else knowing about them, you are giving yourself an excuse to slack off. Without verbally committing to your goal of becoming a high school **state champion**, you are not putting anything on the line. When pride gets damaged it hurts, and no one likes to get hurt. Telling others what your goals are will hold you accountable for your actions and will test your sense of inner pride. When others know what you are setting out to do, your goals become a reality. You will be more motivated to attack unforeseen challenges and will think twice before taking the easy way out.

Sharing with coaches, teammates, parents, and friends that you want to win a high school state title will give them an incentive to help you. When people know you are motivated to win

How to become the next state wrestling champion.

something as demanding and prestigious as a state title, they will want to be a part of it. In general, people look to surround themselves with successful people. Tell the people on your support team your dream of winning a high school state title and watch the help pour in. This will prove to be a key that opens many doors. Do not be shy and do not be ashamed of your goals. Be proud of who you are. Put your pride on the line and make your goals public.

Writing down your goals is a great way to remind yourself of the long-term goal you are working towards. If you are not able to sit down with a piece of paper and write: "I want to win a high school state title in the year 20-- at ---lbs.," then it is not a legitimate goal. Write your dreams down on paper and keep them in a familiar place where you will always see them:

- The mirror in the bathroom
- On your ceiling above your bed
- Inside of your locker
- On your bedroom door
- Inside your wallet

The more you are able to see your goals staring back at you the more you will become attached to them. When goals are fresh on your mind you will be more determined to conquer them. This is a vital step in the goal-setting process.

Taping your goals in one or more of the areas I noted above will remind you of where you are headed. You will be surprised when you start to learn how many great athletes have goals in places they are sure to see everyday. For example, in the movie *Rocky IV*, Rocky keeps a picture of the Russian boxer in the frame of the bathroom mirror. Is this because he likes to gaze at his competition? No, it is because it keeps him determined and focused on crushing his competition and achieving his goal of being the best.

Make a commitment to your goals. Tell as many people as you can about what you are setting out to do. Put your pride on the line with a verbal commitment and make sure that your goals are always readily handy and visible.

"Goals that are not written down are just wishes."
- Unknown

What Happens When My Goals Are Reached?

Anyone who has ever set out to reach a challenging long-term goal can tell you that it is not an easy thing to accomplish. However, you must be prepared for the time when you do accomplish your goal of being a high school **state champion** and know where to go from there.

Figuring out what to do after you have accomplished a goal is easy. If you are committed to being the best, you will strive to reach the next level of excellence. Once you win your first state title the next step is figuring out how you can win your second. But you will not only want to win again, you will want to win in the most dominating fashion possible. Never be satisfied. You must always strive for greatness.

How to become the next state wrestling champion.

If you find yourself winning your first and only state title when you are a senior in high school, your next set of long-term goals will be geared towards accomplishing your lifelong dreams. You will have to figure out what is best for your future outside of high school. There are many avenues to explore and they are all up to you to discover. For now, shoot for that state title and become the champion that I know you can be.

If you do not reach your dreams the first time around, you must not feel sorry for yourself. Dust yourself off and reevaluate where you went wrong. Perhaps you did not set the best performance goals on the way to achieving your long-term goal. Maybe you cheated yourself by missing a few workouts because you were convinced it would not matter in the long run.

Every short-term performance goal and every workout matters; do not take them for granted or take them lightly. If you do not meet your set goals take a step back, reevaluate, and figure out how to fix them.

Do not let falling short of a long-term goal stop you from becoming a champion. You always have opportunities to become great off the mat as well. Continue to set goals, both long and short, until you find yourself accomplishing what you set out to do. Once you find yourself there, start over and begin writing a new plan for your next exciting journey.

"Leaders are made, they are not born. They are made by hard effort, which is

A proven plan that guarantees success.

the price which all of us must pay to achieve any goal that is worth-while."
- *Vincent Lombardi*

Chapter Summary

1. Goal setting is decision making.
2. Goal setting is deciding that you want to accomplish a task and will do whatever it takes to accomplish that task.
3. Goals are the milestones that aid you in your quest towards greatness.
4. Having a goal in mind will force you to progress and get better because, like a road map, it will lead you turn by turn to your ultimate destination: Winning a State Title.
5. Long-term goals are set anywhere from six months to several years in advance.
6. Short-term goals are stepping stones that you set along the way. They are set more frequently than long-term goals.
7. It is crucial that you not only set a goal of becoming a **state champion** wrestler, but that you have other small performance goals along the way.
8. Performance goals are there to help bring you closer to your dream of winning a state title.
9. Anaerobic training goals are intended to help improve the strength of your muscles when they are completely broken down.
10. Aerobic activities are those that condition the heart and body by increasing how well the body takes in and processes oxygen.

How to become the next state wrestling champion.

11. When setting goals for dieting, if you need to, it is incredibly important to make sure that you are losing weight in a healthy manner.
12. You must have performance goals geared towards improving your technique.
13. It is crucial that you do both of the following: tell someone your goals and write them down on paper. This forces you to be committed.

A proven plan that guarantees success.

Step Five

Drilling

The Importance of Drilling

"You've got to think of the 'big things' while you're doing small things, so that all the small things go in the right direction."
- *Alvin Toffler*

When I first started to wrestle in junior high school, drilling technique was the bane of my existence. I could not understand why it was so important. I figured it was more fun to spar than to go through moves half speed because during a match nothing happens half speed. As I progressed with my wrestling, had **One-on-One** training, and began winning matches, I learned the relevancy of drilling. Without it there is no way of knowing what to do during a match. Drilling technique the correct way is one of the most important aspects of becoming a good wrestler. If you are not able to execute a

A proven plan that guarantees success.

technique correctly half speed, in practice, you cannot possibly expect to use it successfully under pressure, in competition.

Drilling is not just "going through the motions." Drilling is done over and over again each practice for a purpose. Your coach does not tell you to drill key positions before practice starts just to keep you busy while he takes attendance. Coaches make their wrestlers drill with hopes that the practiced moves will one day become second nature. By this I mean that important positions and techniques will become ingrained in your mind so the body will follow. You will no longer have to think about techniques before performing them in an adrenaline-riddled match; they will become reactions. After hours of successful drilling, you may find yourself in a scramble situation that calls for you to execute a re-shot on your opponent's legs, and before you realize it, your body will re-shoot on its own. This may be hard for you to comprehend, but trust me, after practicing thousands of hours of drilling throughout my career, I know this to be true.

When thinking about drilling, consider the following quote by Rick Warren. "When you are through improving, you are through [winning]." Apply this to your drilling sessions by substituting the word "improving" with drilling. **"WHEN YOU ARE THROUGH DRILLING YOU ARE THROUGH [WINNING]."** Drilling is synonymous with improvement. Without structured drilling habits your wrestling techniques will remain stagnant and your competition will pass you by. As much as drilling may seem like a chore, it is a crucial part of wrestling that is essential for success at each stage of your career.

Do It Right The First Time

This section on correct drilling skills gives pointers on how to become the perfect driller. Each sub-title describes techniques that I have developed throughout my career by learning from different coaches on all levels. These techniques demand perfection. The only way to perfect them is to do them consistently every time. Do not skip steps when you are feeling lazy by using excuses like "I'll do it later." Excuses create bad habits that are nearly impossible to break.

Each takedown has a set-up: Every time you drill a take-down (double leg, single leg, high crotch, front headlock, throw, etc.), you must have a set-up. A set-up forces your opponent to react, creating an opportunity to perform a take-down. For example, tapping your opponent on the head will put them on their heels for a split second giving you a small window of opportunity to get in on and finish a deep shot.

Practicing takedowns without a set-up is counter-productive to success. You will never take an opponent down without a set-up because your opponent will not be forced to their heels and caught off guard. The lack of a proper set-up gives your opponent an opportunity to counter your attack.

Whether a takedown is clean or results from a scramble, it always develops from an initial set-up. I cannot repeat the phrase **SET-UP** enough times to stress its importance to you. If you want to win a state title, you will have to know how to perform a perfect set-up for every takedown in your arsenal of techniques.

Check and recheck your position: Each time you come to your feet after drilling a takedown, check and recheck your stance. This is a simple skill I learned from watching a clinic given by Tom Brands, an Olympic Gold Medalist. You cannot imagine how many times takedowns that begin from a poor starting position prove to be ineffective during live wrestling.

Correct drilling involves precision in each phase. Stance is the most important. Without a good stance 100% of the time, you are giving your opponent the upper hand. Between each takedown you drill make sure that:

- Your shoulders, knees, and toes are in vertical alignment with each other
- Your feet are at least shoulder width apart
- Your head is up
- The arm that is on the same side of your lead leg is down low for defensive protection
- Your elbows are in and your thumbs are facing the ceiling
- You are bent at the waist with your weight on the balls of your feet

Checking each aspect of your stance will save you a lot of frustration down the road.

Do not be afraid to ask: Do not be afraid to ask your drill partner to change the look he is giving you. By look, I mean stance and lead leg. If you want to practice shooting your high crotch to your left side and your partner is leading his left leg you cannot drill the high crotch to that particular side. Ask your partner to switch his lead. The only way your partner can know what you want to work on is to tell him.

Your partners are there to help you just as you are there to help them. This tip is also helpful after you have scouted your opponent for an upcoming match. If you know your opponent's stance or lead leg, have a partner simulate it and practice the takedowns that will work against that particular style. Your opponent will be very surprised when none of their techniques are successful against you because you have prepared for his particular style.

Chain wrestling: By now I am sure most of you probably heard of the term *chain wrestling*. Chain wrestling means flowing from one move and one finish to the next. It occurs while wrestling on your feet, on top, or on bottom.

It is necessary to drill chain wrestling as often as possible because it will help you decrease the time it takes to perform a second, third, or fourth technique when a primary technique does not work. Your reaction time will get substantially faster by drilling chain wrestling. Here are the steps to drill chain wrestling:

- Tell your drill partner that you want to work on chain wrestling and have them drill actively with you giving 50% resistance.
- The goal of chain wrestling is to mimic wrestling in a match, yet your partner will let you perform and finish technique without a hard fight.
- Hand fight, at 50% resistance, into a position from which you favor attacking.

A proven plan that guarantees success.

- Perform an offensive takedown technique, but allow your partner to defend your attack.
- Return to your feet and check your stance and position.
- Perform a second attack, but once again allow your partner to defend this attack as well.
- Return to your feet and check your stance and position.
- On your third attack finish the takedown to the mat hard, but make sure your partner lands on the mat and finishes in the referee position.
- Return to your feet, check your stance and position, and repeat the latter steps 10-15 times a drill session.
- Drilling chain wrestling in the referee position involves the same disciplines as drilling it on your feet.
- On bottom, force your partner to lift and return you to the mat four times before your fifth escape attempt works.
- While practicing chain wrestling on top, work moving constantly from one pinning combination to the next.
- Allow your partner to return to the referee position between each pinning combination and work at 50% resistance.

In a tough, match-like situation, you will only hit your first move 10% of the time. This is why you must train yourself to be able to connect moves together like links of a chain. Once you are able to implement these aspects into your drilling, you will be on your way to perfecting techniques.

Types Of Drilling

Drilling not only applies to technique but to all facets of wrestling. You may not realize that working on speed, quickness, and strength are also forms of drilling. They are just as important as drilling techniques. The faster you are able to move your feet and react, the better off you will be. Apply the same skills to speed, quickness, and strength drills that you apply to drilling techniques. Some drills that you should familiarize yourself with are:

- Running with high knees
- Kicking your butt with your heels at a high frequency
- Jumping rope
- Squat jumps
- Rope climbing
- Short sprints
- Hand fighting
- Shadow wrestling
- Drilling takedowns and hand fighting with an ADAM dummy

Make sure you apply technique-drilling skills to each of these complementary drills. Check your position on each sprint or each squat jump. Have a partner change the time you have to complete a series of sprints. Tie one speed drill into the next, or add a strength drill to the end of a jump rope session to mimic drilling chain wrestling. Force yourself to perform each drill correctly with a high level of intensity, especially when you are tired at the end of practice. Training through fatigue is great preparation, physically

A proven plan that guarantees success.

and mentally, for learning how to properly execute your skills during a match.

"Even if you are on the right track, you'll get run over if you just sit there."
- Will Rogers

Chapter Summary

1. Drilling technique the correct way every time is one of the most important aspects of becoming a good wrestler.
2. Drilling is synonymous with improvement.
3. Every takedown requires a set-up.
4. Check and recheck your position.
5. Do not be afraid to ask your drill partner to do something specific for you to practice a particular technique.
6. Chain wrestling allows you to practice perfecting several techniques in common sequential order, as they would be used in a match situation.
7. Make sure you apply technique-drilling skills, such as doing things correctly every time and always checking for good position, to every complementary drill included in your workout.
8. If you do not drill techniques or complementary drill correctly, it is senseless to do them at all.

Step Six
(V.P.) Visualization Plus

What is Visualization Plus?

Professional athletes do it. College and high school wrestlers do it. Teachers, businessmen, and coaches even do it. I am talking about painting a vivid mental picture of your goals and fulfilling your dreams inside of your mind. More specifically, I am talking about a process in which you can sense every detail of wrestling the perfect match by using mental imagery. I like to call this technique of seeing and hearing **Visualization Plus**.
     Once you have done all of the weightlifting, all of the running, and all of the drilling, you must complete one last task of the **Working Smart** process. Close your eyes, paint a mental image, and actually practice seeing your goals evolve into reality. When practicing **V.P.**, you are combining imagined sights and sounds to create a vivid image of accomplishing your goals.
     Throughout my years of competition I have

A proven plan that guarantees success.

noticed most elite athletes believe mental preparation is just as important as physical preparation. I have discovered wrestlers who compete at a very high level believe that a very high percentage of their performance can be attributed to mental preparation. Many athletes have the ability to reach the level of physical preparation necessary to become a champion. However, those who are incapable of preparing mentally will find themselves unable to successfully utilize their physical training when it counts. If you do not practice seeing and hearing yourself winning the championship match at the state tournament, it will never happen.

The climb to the state title is oftentimes full of devastating setbacks that could leave you seconds short of capturing your state title. It is imperative that you practice forming a mental picture in your mind where you see yourself standing tall with your hand raised. Hear the chanting and cheering of ecstatic fans as your name is called in victory.

How to Visualize Winning

At this point you might be asking some of the following questions: How in the world do I envision an entire match inside my mind? What is a mental image and how do I imagine it as reality?

V.P. is a process that requires deep concentration and focus. If you are not able to concentrate with a clear mind, **V.P.** will not work for you. The best way to practice is to find a spot or room where you are the most comfortable; a location that is quiet, calming, and free from

How to become the next state wrestling champion.

distractions. Relaxing in front of a loud television is not a quiet place, so be sure to steer clear of such distractions.

Once you are in a quite location, and are comfortable, you can start to practice **V.P.** techniques.

- Start by taking in eight to ten deep breaths that begin deep in your belly and end high in your chest.
- Take your time inhaling through your mouth and exhaling through your nose. Exhaling should take twice as long as inhaling to allow ample time to get as relaxed as possible.
- Now concentrate on relaxing each muscle of your body one at a time. Start from your toes and finish at the top of your head.
- Release all of the tension that you might be feeling. Let each of your muscles sag to the ground as you feel the weight from stress float away from your body.
- Feel a calming sensation come over your body.
- Concentrate on your ultimate goal: Winning the **state championship.**
- Give yourself plenty of time, at least ten minutes, to see and hear the most detailed aspects of your wrestling.
- Perfect each match leading up to the championship.
- It is important that you do not rush any part of the **V.P.** process. They are all equally important.

Once you can see yourself standing on the mat staring directly at your opponent, you are ready to begin wrestling. **WARNING: YOU MIGHT**

A proven plan that guarantees success.

START TO GET EXCITED SEEING YOURSELF WINNING A STATE TITLE AND YOUR BREATHING MIGHT BEGIN TO INTENSIFY. YOUR MUSCLES MAY ALSO BEGIN TO TIGHTEN. DO NOT ALLOW THIS TO HAPPEN. RELAX YOUR BREATHING THROUGH CONCENTRATION AND REMAIN CALM. THE ONLY WAY YOU WILL WIN A STATE TITLE IS IF YOU ARE RELAXED AND COMFORTABLE.
See yourself shaking your opponent's hand and feel the grip you give it. Feel the blood stop flowing to your opponent's fingers because of your bone-crunching grip.

You must be able to hear the whistle blow, and each subsequent whistle, as you begin to wrestle. Open your ears and hear the roaring of your fans' thundering down from the arena seats. Picture the techniques you have mastered that will be essential to winning your state title. Do not only think of completing a move, but also see yourself complete each step of the move. The set-up, the shot, and the finish are all equally important parts of a takedown, so do not skip over them.

Feel your opponent's hands clutching the back of you leg as you fight off his shot. Listen to him gasp for air as you crush his lungs while thrusting your hips down onto his head, ripping apart his grip on your leg, and moving around behind to score a two-point takedown. In the midst of all the action, you must also be listening for your coach's voice yelling advice that could be crucial as you fight to finish each technique. Always keep an acute sense of hearing while practicing **V.P.**. The sounds of victory will make winning your state title that much more real and exciting.

Work your way through the second and third period, but do not stop there. You must also practice seeing yourself in an overtime period followed by a sudden death period. See yourself fighting every second to either escape from your opponent's grip or successfully holding down your opponent during the thirty-second sudden death. **IT IS CRUCIAL THAT YOU USE YOUR IMAGINATION TO PUT YOURSELF IN EVERY POSSIBLE POSITION THAT YOU MAY ENCOUNTER DURING A MATCH.** Practice choosing both top and bottom in the second period or even deferring until the third period. See yourself react to a variety of possible circumstances. Decide where to put your hands and where to move your feet.

The most important part of **V.P.** is to not only see and hear yourself in each position, but to see and hear yourself winning each position. Never, and I mean never, see yourself lose a position. **V.P.** is completely useless if you are not the winner at the end of a scramble or the end of the match.

V.P. is a technique that will allow you to improve your wrestling, just as drilling does. You do not drill techniques poorly to do them wrong during a match, so never visualize yourself losing.

If you are able to see yourself winning the **state championship** title, if you are able to wrestle the perfect match in your mind, you will be on your way to winning in reality. Leave no step of **V.P.** overlooked. It is a process that requires lots of practice. This is not a technique that can be mastered all at once. You must find a quite location, relax yourself through deep breathing, stay relaxed, and actually see and hear yourself winning every position of your perfect state title match.

When And Where To Visualize

Practice **V.P.** techniques as often as possible. Once you have mastered them in a comfortable, quiet location you will be able to use them anywhere. As soon as you successfully attempt to see and hear yourself wrestling the perfect mental match, it will become second nature.

Here are just a few of the places and times I used **V.P.**:

- Upon waking up in the morning or after a nap
- After practice while cooling down or stretching
- On the bus to and from competition
- During study hall in school after all my work was completed
- Before a match
- Whenever I had spare time and wanted to see myself becoming a champion

Ask yourself which is easier: giving a speech in front of a class without any practice, or giving a speech that you have rehearsed twenty times? My experiences with public speaking tell me that practicing it twenty times always produces better results. The same holds true for visualizing your state title match. The more frequently you are able to visualize yourself winning a state title, the easier it will be when you are actually wrestling.

Experience wins when it comes to high-stress and high-profile matches such as the **state**

How to become the next state wrestling champion.

championship match. While your opponents are at home mindlessly watching television, you can be at home seeing yourself brutalizing them in the state finals. If you can see and hear it, then it will become reality. Ask yourself whether you want to be the lazy one or the one winning?

See yourself winning, see the perfect match, and go win the **state championship** match that I know you can win. Can you not hear and see all the people congratulating you as the gold medal is placed around your neck? I certainly can!

"When your opponent is bigger, faster, stronger, train harder, longer, smarter."
- H. Jackson Brown, Jr.

Chapter Summary

1. In successful, elite athletes, a very high percentage of performance can be attributed to mental preparation.
2. **Visualization Plus** is a process in which you are able to see and hear in your mind every second of wrestling the perfect match.
3. You must be able to close your eyes, paint a mental image, and actually see your goals become a reality.
4. **Visualization Plus** is a process that requires deep concentration and focus.
5. The best way to focus and concentrate is to find a spot or room where you are the most comfortable.
6. As you breathe slowly, begin the **Visualization Plus** process by concentrating on

A proven plan that guarantees success.

    relaxing each muscle of your body one fiber at a time.
7. Do not rush your visualization.
8. Concentrate on your ultimate goal: Winning the **state championship**.
9. Listen for every sound that will be heard in the arena while you are wrestling.
10. Practice **Visualization Plus** techniques as often as possible. The more you can practice **Visualization Plus** and the more you are able to see yourself winning a state title, the more successful you will be.

Camps And Clinics

This chapter on camps and clinics is geared towards you, the wrestler, and your parents. I say this because you will notice that the advice I am going to give often requires the help of an adult. Oftentimes you will need transportation and financial assistance to participate in a camp or clinic, so it is important that both you and your parents read this chapter.

Dozens of new wrestling camps and clinics start up every year all over the country. Why? They are an excellent way for colleges and schools to generate additional revenue while students are either on a break or on summer vacation. Schools already have the facilities, the empty gymnasiums, and a built-in coaching staff. With minimal advertising geared towards eager wrestlers wanting to get that extra edge, camps and clinics are a gold mine for them.

Is it a mistake to go away to camp or to attend a clinic? No, but you do need to know exactly what you are paying for and what you are getting yourself into. You must ask yourself why you are going to a camp or a clinic and what you want to get out of it. Be honest with your answers because attending a camp is a large financial investment for parents, and an even larger personal commitment on your part. If you do not want to go to a particular wrestling camp or clinic in the first place, I can guarantee that you will not only have a miserable time, you will not learn anything.

At this point, it is important to share some of my own personal experiences with wrestling camps and clinics I have been involved with in past years.

When I first began wrestling I thought to myself, what better way to learn than from the best? I made sure that each camp or clinic I attended had highly qualified staffs with pages of credentials. The clinicians I sought out had earned a place among the finest wrestlers both past and present. Judging from their credentials alone, I thought I would automatically become a better wrestler. Like I said earlier, **TO BE THE BEST YOU HAVE TO WORK WITH THE BEST**. With this idea in mind, I went to camps and clinics in West Virginia and Colorado, and everywhere in-between.

Below are the most important lessons I learned from my experiences with camps and clinics. Once again, be aware that the advice I am giving is not only for you, but also for your parents.

Lessons Learned

Many large camps and clinics do not offer the **One-On-One** instruction that I believe to be essential to winning a high school state title, so you must create your own **One-On-One** coaching environment. To create your own **One-on-One** atmosphere, get to sessions early and stay after they are finished. It is easier to set up personal

How to become the next state wrestling champion.

One-On-One instruction if you talk with the clinicians and counselors about scheduling individual time either before or after a session.

Clinicians and counselors enjoy the fact that you are interested in their wrestling style and it usually boosts their egos a little bit when campers request further assistance. Believe me when I tell you that clinicians and counselors want to help. Get to know them well and do not be afraid to approach them.

Even though the lack of **One-on-One** instruction was the first disappointing lesson I learned about large group camps and clinics, I forced myself to work around the big numbers. I had my dad arrange for some **One-on-One** instruction prior to the beginning of a camp or clinic. It's like the old adage, "Ask for help and you shall receive."

You do not have to travel hundreds of miles and spend endless hours in a car to find a good wrestling camp or clinic. Most wrestlers can find excellent opportunities in their hometown or in surrounding areas. The only summer camps I attended after not receiving any personal instruction at the large-group camps were in my local area. They were usually held at small, local colleges or high schools and some were run through city park districts. After I had earned third place as a sophomore and won the state title as a junior, I helped out as an attending clinician and worked with other wrestlers who were not as advanced. This is just one of the benefits to winning a state title before your senior year.

My next piece of advice will help you get all you can out of wrestling camps and clinics. Do not simply sign up for a camp or clinic, send in your money, and hope that the camp or clinic you have picked will be a good experience. You or

A proven plan that guarantees success.

your parents must call the director of the camp or clinic personally and find out exactly what will be taught, who is going to be instructing, and what their policies are on parents viewing some of the sessions. If you or your parents do not like a particular clinician or certain policy, then you should look for a more suitable camp or clinic.

By doing your research, you will find out enough information to ensure a quality camp or clinic experience that is worth the financial commitment. Contacting the director of the camp or clinic is the best way to get the information you need in to decide if the one you chose will suit your needs. Also, by talking with directors and making personal contacts, you will be laying the groundwork for future requests of **One-On-One** instruction that will improve your wrestling the most during the spring and summer months.

Often, you will find that there is a lot of "slack-off" time and sometimes overcrowding at wrestling camps and clinics. In an effort to turn as much profit as possible, directors tend to over-reserve spots for campers. The lack of supervision makes it easy for you, as a camper, to lose concentration. This especially holds true if the camp or clinic has a poor student-to-teacher ratio.

I am not saying you and every other wrestler at a crowded camp or clinic will spend all your time goofing off, but kids will be kids. In life, and in wrestling, you will only get out of it what you put into it. With this in mind, it is essential that you investigate camp and clinic numbers prior to enrollment. Beware of overcrowded conditions.

Next, if you decide to go to a camp and want to be a **state champion,** you must skip technique-based camps and clinics, and commit yourself to the intensive camp and clinic experience. Do not be scared off by the term "intensive." Although it may sound harsh, it is a proven fact that **you must be intense if you want to succeed and win a state title.**

"Intensive camps" or "training camps" teach technique at a pace that enables you to drill moves hard and practice them under match like conditions. The more hard drilling and match experience you have, the better off you will be in the long run. Experience kills and in order to win a high school state title you must have plenty of experience in your back pocket.

A Guide To Camps and Clinics

Attending a summer wrestling camp or clinic is by no means an easy task. There are many factors to take into account when considering what to pack, what not to pack, and what is expected of you once you arrive at camp. I have put together a list of items and helpful hints that will make your camping experience smooth and enjoyable. This list will take out all of the guess work of camp preparation and allow you more time to focus on the task at hand, which is working toward your **state championship**. When leaving for camp make a photocopy of this list and check off each bulleted item as you complete it. Double check and recheck the double check to make sure you have not forgotten one of the essentials.

A proven plan that guarantees success.

What to Pack For Workout Sessions

- Work out gear: t-shirts, shorts, underwear, socks, sweats. *Pack as much gear as possible because of the multiple daily sessions.*
- Shoes: running and wrestling
- Head gear
- Mouth guard
- Athletic bag: essential for carrying your shoes and extra gear to and from sessions.
- Notebook or journal: use to record key points of technique, new technique, or tips from clinicians. *Do not forget this valuable information by not writing it down.*

What To Bring For Housing

- Bedding: sheets and blanket and/or sleeping bag, pillow
- Toiletries: soap, shampoo, deodorant, toothbrush, toothpaste, lotion for skin (skin gets very dry from a lot of wrestling), any other personal care items you need
- Towels: at least two towels due to frequent showering (shower once after each workout)
- Shower shoes: protects feet from "athletes foot"
- Laundry bag and detergent: a bag to keep dirty workout gear in and detergent if you need to wash your gear. *Make sure to bring enough change to work the coin laundry machines if needed.*

How to become the next state wrestling champion.

- Fan: most camps are held during the summer months without air conditioning. A fan is essential to staying comfortable.
- Alarm clock/watch: you are responsible for waking up on time. *Do not forget an alarm clock of some type.*
- Extra spending money: bring a little extra money if you can afford it. Oftentimes there are video games and such to use in the housing facilities during down time.

Tricks Of The Trade

- Arrive early for camp registration. This is a hectic time for everyone. Plan ahead and start off on the right foot.
- If you drive yourself to camp make sure to give your car keys to the camp directory immediately. This will ensure that you will not run into any sort of problem later in the camp with regards to your car and transportation.
- Eat all the meals offered throughout the day. Plenty of energy is essential to getting all you can out of each workout.
- Stay hydrated by drinking plenty of water at each meal, during sessions, and after sessions. Dehydration will cause fatigue to set in quickly.
- If you want to order extra food at night (i.e. pizza or fast food), do so early. Counselors do not appreciate last-minute food runs.
- Respect other campers (male and female). Disrespecting others is a sure way to get sent home early. *I have seen this happen numerous times.*

A proven plan that guarantees success.

- To be early is to be on time. To be on time is to be late. To be late is to be never. Arrive at each session early. If you need to get a body part taped plan ahead and allow for extra time.
- Never wear your wrestling shoes to a session. Always change shoes once you are at the practice facility.
- Ask clinicians and counselors questions. You must be a sponge for knowledge if you want to get the most out of your camping experience.
- Pack early on the last day and be prepared to check out on time. The earlier the better. No one likes to wait.

Be sure to photocopy this list of tips and camping necessities before leaving for camp. I have seen every situation imaginable at camps from both a camper's and a counselor's perspective. By following my guidelines you should have a smooth, memorable camping experience.

Chapter Summary

1. You must ask yourself why you are going to a camp or clinic and what you want to get out of it.
2. **BEWARE:** Many camps and clinics do not offer the **One-On-One** instruction that I believe is essential to winning a high school state title.
3. Get to know the clinicians and do not be afraid to approach them.

How to become the next state wrestling champion.

4. You do not have to travel hundreds of miles, spending endless hours in a car to find a good wrestling camp or clinic. You can find great opportunities in your hometown or in surrounding areas.
5. You or your parent must call the camp or clinic director personally before committing financially.
6. It is essential that you investigate potentially over-crowded camp and clinic conditions and avoid them.
7. If you want to be a **state champion**, you must skip technique-based camps and clinics, and jump right into the intensive experience.

A proven plan that guarantees success.

The Wrap-Up

"Think highly of yourself because the world takes you at your own estimate."
- Unknown

    Well, you made it. You have read through my plan cover-to-cover, and now know just what it takes to be the best. The road to a state title is not an easy road by any means. The journey to the top of the podium is only for those willing to make the commitment. It is only for those who have enough courage to adopt a plan and put these essential steps to work for them.
    Since you have read my book I know that you are a wrestler who yearns to be great. You have the thirst for competition and the dedication to win. You are hungry for success and will let nothing stand between you and your state title. I embrace each of these qualities because they are exactly what champions are made of.
    Reading this book for the first time is just the beginning of your wonderful journey. To gain a complete understanding of what it takes to grab the gold medal, you must read through this book several times. Become a wrestling scholar. Learn

A proven plan that guarantees success.

every detail to perfection; it will make all the difference.

The information provided is not something that can be learned instantaneously. It is information that requires hours and hours of studying. Allow it to seep deep into your brain by reading it thoroughly several times. Review the summaries at the end of each step and memorize the key points. They are key points for a reason and should not be taken lightly.

I wish you the best of luck on your journey to ownership of a state title. I hope you have the same unforgettable experiences that I had on my journey to the top of the podium. You must cherish each moment of glory and know that there is no greater feeling in the world than achieving your goals.

Shoot for the stars and do not settle for anything less than greatness. Adopt a winning wrestling style and allow confidence to flow through your veins like surges of electricity. Once you start off on your journey to the top of the podium and begin to model yourself after my plan you will never want to look back. Become the champion that I know you can be. Do not let any obstacles stand in your way of winning. Use the plan outlined in this book to carry you through the ups and downs associated with striving for lofty goals. Good luck, it is time to get to work!

To close this guide, I have included a personal experience of my parents in the stands during both of my **state championship** matches. Feel the emotions that they felt. Imagine how it was for them to see their son achieving greatness and what it will be like for your parents. Even more so, imagine what it felt like for me to end my journey with a second state title in front of the people I love most. Enjoy their story and take away with you a message of success.

The View From the Top

We actually got some great seats on finals night. Unfortunately, there are no individual seating assignments for the State meet, so when the doors of Assembly Hall open, everyone rushes in hoping to get the best seats. Luckily, a friend of ours, Joe Drendal, had somehow managed to save us a few seats in the first row. The only problem was there just weren't enough seats for everyone who wanted to sit up close, including the coaches' wives. I felt sorry for them because they had brought their small children with them, and were unable to sit up front where they belonged. After all, it was their husbands/dads who were out on the mats coaching our wrestlers.

Was I nervous? Absolutely. I normally walk around a lot, pacing, because I can't sit still for very long during a meet. This particular night was even more difficult. One thing that was really bothering me was the fact that a lot of people were saying, "It's in the bag, he won't have any problem, no sweat." If there is one thing I have learned in sports and in life, it is not to count your chickens before they hatch. I was confident in the win but you must never, never underestimate your opponent.

Look, I just wanted the whole thing to be over with so we could get one state title under our belt and move on with our lives. The year before Chuck had finished third in the 145 lbs weight class, but at least for me, this particular year's pressure was altogether different.

A proven plan that guarantees success.

Although I had been to the **state championship** meet a few times in the past, on this specific night, the Grand March was utterly fantastic. The music and fan support sent chills up my spine and tears of joy down my face. Hearing my son's name being announced, "In AA, at 152 lbs., undefeated Charles Martelli," was a rush I just cannot put into words. Even now, just remembering and visualizing the ringing of those words over the loud speaker brings tears to my eyes as I write. It is a precious moment, the state finals, an experience reserved for a very few. It is an experience you will never forget. Talk about a natural high; this was it!

When the wrestling started I went out in the hall, found a chair, and watched most of the matches on televisions set up around the outer concourse of the arena. It was quiet in the hallway, almost like a ghost town. As I sat there pondering the past, everything we had gone through the last few years, all the ups and downs and all the people we had met, went through my mind. All of them were great memories.

Time seemed to be standing still. Then all of a sudden, the hundred and forty-five place matches ended. I got up, went inside and sat down next to my wife. Everything our family, coaches, and supporters had put into wrestling had come down to this final match. Quite frankly, Chuck looked very tough, confident and strong, like a man on a mission for a state title. It was time to perform and he was ready. I could see it in his eyes; there was no way he was going to let this win slip through his hands.

As parents, Linda and I were probably more uptight than he was. The match took a long time to get through because there were a lot of injury time outs, etc. Chuck took the lead and never let

How to become the next state wrestling champion.

up. He was relentless. His plan was to get in his opponent's face from the first whistle until the last. That is his style and that is exactly what he did winning the match 8-4.

Afterward, my wife and I went down on the competition floor to take pictures. We hugged him for a long time. We all cried tears of joy and relief that it was over. I told him how much I loved him and could not stop trembling. It was a tremendous experience for everyone involved.

A newspaper reporter asked me how it felt to have my son win a state title. All I could manage to reply with was, "It feels great to win it and to get all of the pressure off."

One section of the arena was filled with our friends, teammates, and well-wishers who came from all over. I'm very grateful to everyone that was there.

Working your way up and being in a **state championship** final is an event you just don't want to miss. But getting there a second time and winning twice is simply incredible.

The night of Charles's second state championship match was a little different from the first one. Once again our family was sitting in the front row. This time I managed to stay in my seat for the entire meet. For me, this was a very large step in watching my son compete. My nervousness showed, but I was not outwardly out of control. Chuck's final high school match, the championship match, took all of one minute and thirteen seconds. He hit a quick inside fireman's carry into back points that his opponent never saw coming. As the referee slapped his hand on the mat, signaling a pin, the crowd just exploded.

Once again, we had a huge following from our area and they made us feel really special. It has been four and a half years since the doors at

A proven plan that guarantees success.

Assembly Hall closed ending a great high school experience for our whole family. Frankly I'm glad it's all over, but at the same time very thankful that we are able to have such wonderful experiences to look back on.

The pressure of Chuck's last season was much more intense and difficult to handle. You are going to find out that most people want the underdog to win and in our situation they wanted our son to fall flat on his face. So be prepared! I am not talking about close friends. They will always be with you no matter what. But there are a lot of people out there that are jealous and envious of what your child has accomplished. They have no idea of what **Working Smart** is or what it takes to become a champion. They never will.

The pressure is different the second time around. It's more intense, more difficult to handle because the stakes are a lot higher. As your winning streak continues and as records start falling, you are reminded of it on a daily basis, if not by a well-wisher then by the morning newspaper or a television report. I'm not complaining, I am simply telling you to be prepared for success.

Heaven forbid you have a close match. If you do not get a pin or win by more than ten points a lot of people will think something must be wrong. Everyone tends to forget that we are dealing with 17 year-old kids and his or her families, not professional athletes. Basically, I am very grateful for all we have, but just remember to be prepared for every possible pitch they can throw at you.

Kids, watch how and what you say to the media. Reporters seek out controversial stories and love disagreement. They can take a simple

How to become the next state wrestling champion.

comment and embellish it out of context. For example, Charles happened to mention that one of his goals was to pin his way through the **state championship** series: regional, sections, and the state tournament. Every other week there was something written about this comment. The press just would not let it go. Personally, I thought it was something great to shoot for, but also something that the whole world did not need to know about.

He did end up pinning everyone at the Regional and Sectional Tournaments and pinned the last two of his four opponents down state. This included the record-setting one minute and thirteen second pin in the 160 lb. final match.

Here is a little sidebar that I know you will get a kick out of: We didn't realize that the wrestler Chuck pinned in the final match was the same boy that had pinned him in his very first wrestling match back in sixth grade. I remember being upset back then, but as you can imagine, I am more than satisfied with how things turned out in the end.

How's the view at the top, you ask? Well, it's second to none. You've taken a great step towards reaching your ultimate destination in the best way possible, by investing in this book. We have been where you are going, and all I can say at this point is:

Someone has to be the next state champion. Why not you?

A proven plan that guarantees success.

How to become the next state wrestling champion.

Quick Order Form

Online orders: www.statechampwrestling.com

Postal Orders: State Champion Wrestling Co.
1404 West Street
Naperville, IL 60563

------------- **Tear Out and Send with Payment** -----------

Please mark quantity of desired product(s):

Book w/Free Motivational Poster ($15.95) Qty.____
Shipping and Handling $4.95
Add $1.00 for each additional book ordered.

Sub Total $_____ + $ S/H= Total $_____

Name: _____
Address: _____
City: _____ State: _____ Zip: _____
Telephone: _____
Email address: _____
Payment: Check   Credit Card
                          Visa   Master Card

***** **Please do not send CASH** *****

Name on card: _____
Card number: _____
Exp. date: _____

A proven plan that guarantees success.